ROCK SPORT

D0012593

ROCK SPORT

Tools, Training, and Techniques for Climbers

JOHN FORREST GREGORY

STACKPOLE BOOKS

Published by
STACKPOLE BOOKS
Cameron and Kelker Streets
P.O. Box 1831
Harrisburg, PA 17105

Printed in the United States of America

First Edition

10   9   8   7   6   5   4

Illustrations by Montague Lord.
Cover photo by Mike Whitman: "Cascading Crystal Kaleidoscope"
at the Shawangunks, New York.

Table on p. 54 appears by permission of Timothy J. Setnicka and Appalachian
Mountain Club Books, Boston.

Library of Congress Cataloging-in-Publication Data
Gregory, John Forrest.
    Rock sport : tools, training, and techniques for climbers / John
  Forrest Gregory.
        p.   cm.
    Includes index.
    ISBN 0-8117-2296-1
    1. Rock climbing.   I. Title.
  GV200.2.G74   1989
  796.5′223′028 – dc19   88-32368
                                                      CIP

CONTENTS

LIST OF ILLUSTRATIONS

ACKNOWLEDGMENTS

A lot of people helped make this book possible. I prepared the original manuscript to collect the material we taught at the Seneca Rocks Climbing School. Bob Shimizu keyed the entire thing into an IBM mainframe, and with the help of Lisa Peoples, Jane Waterman, and Teri Hallinger, we turned it into something presentable. My friends saw me through three years of additions and corrections, until Sally Atwater of Stackpole Books recognized our efforts. Bob, Jane, Bill Repetto, Raoul LeMat, Jim Borton, and Craig Miller helped with the photos, and John Markwell provided many pictures. John Bercaw was generous with his advice for the chapter on training.

AN IMPORTANT NOTE TO READERS

This book contains much useful information about the sport of rock climbing. Before engaging in this potentially hazardous sport, however, you must do more than read a book.

The sport requires skill, concentration, physical strength and endurance, proper equipment, knowledge of fundamental principles and techniques, and unwavering commitment to your own safety and that of your companions.

The publisher and author obviously cannot be responsible for your safety. Because rock climbing entails the risk of serious and even fatal injury, we emphasize that you should not begin climbing except under expert supervision. No book can substitute for proper training and experience under the guidance and supervision of a qualified teacher.

INTRODUCTION

The problem in writing a free-climbing text is where to start. What is very basic to some climbers may be a revelation to others. Techniques and tools vary from area to area. To be on the safe side, I will risk repeating some of the fundamentals, and some ideas may appear more than once in the text, to give some unity in a step-by-step approach to a subject that is basically a process, not a hierarchical body of knowledge.

After a look at the game called climbing, we will examine definable skills, which should be mastered before any roped climbing is attempted. When teaching, I spend a good deal of time going over these skills until I am satisfied that students can perform them without fail and have a clear understanding of what they are doing and why.

Next, the belay system as a whole is presented. The finer points of the act of belaying are covered, with an eye toward making the most of the available tools. Rope management in lead climbing will be discussed here. Some of the theory behind the belay will be examined, and this will go a long way toward explaining choices of particular practices over others.

Fourth, we look at anchor points. This includes a discussion of both belay stance and running belay points. Natural protection, nuts, pitons, bolts, and the tools of free climbing are examined.

Fifth, tactics of lead climbing and options in specific situations are presented. These are the "what if" questions.

The sixth chapter deals with descent — by all means, both in control and totally out of control.

Next is an evaluation of currently available equipment, from the perspective of how various items can be used for the techniques just described.

Finally, a new subject: physical training for rock climbing. We focus on what is best and safest, given the latest information in this fast-changing field. Injury prevention is an important concern.

Probably the best way to use this book is to thumb through it first, looking at the illustrations and finding the tools, techniques, and terminology you are already familiar with. Then go back, read it through, and concentrate on the stuff you didn't know.

A word about sex. Climbers come in two sexes and any number of preferences. They all lead or climb second or solo for the same reasons, and they all share the same fears. Nevertheless, the male pronoun is used in the text as a stylistic convenience—to avoid clumsy sentences and any judgments about who does what with whom.

1

CLIMBING TODAY

How do you explain climbing? The public, fascinated by the incredible spectacle of human beings ascending sheer rock walls, has always considered it an exercise for the mentally unbalanced. Contemporary climbers may cherish this lunatic image, even as they steadfastly refute it, at least in their own minds. If you want to die, they say, try bullfighting or drive a taxi — don't take up climbing.

Climbing has been a sport for more than a hundred years, yet until recently it had only a handful of practitioners. Since the 1970s it has gone through explosive growth. Its popularity hasn't declined as the baby boomers age, or now that stomping around in lug-soled boots has become passé. Climbers used to be college-aged; now they start much younger. Serious adrenaline addicts used to disappear from the local crags, usually after three years. They didn't get beyond a certain level of skill, so they quit. Now climbers tend to leave for a while, whenever some other aspect of their lives demands priority, but then they return, maybe changing the game a bit and finding new ways to enjoy this lifetime sport.

Climbers used to be exclusively male; now a slight majority of new climbers are women. There are no boundaries to women's role in the sport: climbing has so many variables that it does not reward any one type of physique.

The appeal of climbing to all these people may lie in the fact that it is one of the last forms of pure achievement. Progress is self-evident, and you can't fake it. A good resume and the right connections don't help a bit. To climb, you have to empty your mind of the day-to-day bull and focus on the task at hand. All of the little problems of modern life disappear when you deal with basic things like gravity. When you climb, you get to be in complete control — a feeling many of us don't experience in the rest of our lives. Besides, it's comparatively cheap, and you play by your own rules, so it beats the hell out of trying to find a little hole in a golf course.

Climbing is also a wonderful combination of mental and physical effort. Working out moves that are difficult for you, no matter what the level of difficulty, is like a simultaneous exercise in chess and gymnastics. On extreme climbs the moves are actually memorized, or wired, and you can go through the sequence with all the grace and beauty of a dancer in a ballet.

Life sport

There are different types of climbs, and various styles of climbing; goals and environment are what distinguish them. Your goal may be to climb at a certain level of difficulty, or to reach the summit, or to do both. The environment may range from a small rock outcrop to a peak of Himalayan proportions.

So pick the style and level of commitment that suit you. The sport is what you choose to make it. Once you learn the basics, your participation is limited only by time and, to a much lesser degree, money.

Basic skills can get you to some of the most beautiful places on earth. No words have adequately described the feeling of climbing to a mountain summit. Backpacking can have new goals. Even a family vacation can be more interesting. There are a surprising number of

2

climbing areas, so you can combine some time on the rocks with other pursuits. Las Vegas, for example, has large cliffs right outside town. The Caribbean island of St. Thomas has a set of cliffs, complete with tanned rock jocks. Sorry, Hawaii is volcanic crud, but Rio de Janeiro is built around sheer rock walls. If you're ducking icy winds and sleet, the sun may be shining at Hueco Tanks in Texas, the mountains of Arizona, Cabo San Lucas in Baja California, or Joshua Tree National Monument in the Mojave Desert. The high country of the Rockies and the Sierra Nevada can be the best cure for a hot summer in the city.

Local crags can be a surprisingly beautiful antidote to the urban rat race. In Washington, D.C., where I live, I can be climbing just half an hour after leaving my office on Capitol Hill. Washington's beltway is little more than a mile away from Carderock, but the wildlife don't seem to know it. When you're on the cliffs along the banks of the Potomac, aircraft noise is the only hint that you're near a major city.

Some evenings you have the place to yourself. Fish rise to feed on the surface in the fading light and are in turn stalked by herons, ospreys, and kingfishers. A beaver or otter may swim by, and deer appear atop the cliffs. The river runs roughly east to west, so sunsets in the gorge are an experience. Many times you leave with a feeling of rare privilege and peace, something the rich and powerful a few miles away would envy.

It is yours for the taking, and you can get it near any number of cities. Boston has Quincy Quarries, L.A. has Stoney Point, Berkeley has Indian Rock. There are hundreds of climbs within easy reach of Chattanooga and Las Vegas. Denver, Tucson, and San Diego have nearby climbing areas as well.

The after-work group often has an almost clubby atmosphere. But even the people who have climbed together for years are not unwelcoming to newcomers. Weekends in the spring and fall can get a bit crowded, if not downright weird, with military-style rappelers descending face-first, and Boy Scouts with mystery knots. They don't often get hurt, but it may be sheer luck.

What's going on

Some people start climbing by scrambling up a boulder field, but many first see real climbers at a place like Carderock or Stoney Point and want to try it for themselves. Bouldering and top roping are the way to begin.

Let's try some definitions before some eyes glaze over out there:

Bouldering. You climb without a rope, near the ground if you're prudent.

Top roping. A climbing rope runs through an anchor at the top of the cliff to the climber. As he ascends, a second person, the belayer, stands at the bottom and takes in the other end of the rope; falls are immediately caught.

Direct aid. You commit body weight to an anchor to rest or to make progress.

Free climbing. You go up without direct aid.

Solo. You are climbing alone, roped or unroped, aid or free.

Belay. You attach the rope to a fixed point — yourself and some inert anchor — and thus protect the climber's progress. As a noun, the word refers to the anchor.

Third classing. In the American rating system, it means free climbing without belays. An unroped free solo would be third classing.

Lead climbing. The leader climbs (free or with direct aid), trailing the rope; his second feeds out rope while belaying. The leader places intermediate points of protection, then establishes a higher belay and takes in rope as the second climbs up to him, removing the protection as he goes.

When you do everything right, top roping is about as safe as anything gets in life. This doesn't mean you aren't responsible for your own safety. Lots of people *don't* do things right, and some people who really do know better still make mistakes. Climbing can be dangerous, and mistakes have serious consequences.

To minimize mistakes, the first rule in climbing is simplicity. Do the simplest thing that ensures safety. More complicated ways may be safe until you screw up one detail the four-thousandth time you do

A double bowline secures this 11mm static rope low around a substantial tree. A figure-eight on a bight, or loop, is backed up with an overhand knot. The carabiner gates are reversed and opposed. Old 1-inch tubular webbing has been threaded over the rope to protect it from abrasion. Attach the climbing rope, lower the 'biners over the edge of the cliff, and you're ready to go.

it, and then you are going to be just as dead as a rank amateur. This isn't compound interest; you don't build up credit because you did everything right yesterday. Every time you tie into a rope, you are playing for all the marbles.

Belaying for beginners

So you go to the local rocks and start bouldering. Before long someone in need of a belay will take a chance on you. What will get you accepted by other climbers is not just your enthusiasm for the sport — they also have to have confidence in you as a belayer. If they don't, they'll find someone else. Remember, this isn't tennis. If the belayer forgets why he's there, his partner doesn't just lose the match, he could lose his life. People have been needlessly injured while top roping, often because the belayer just wasn't paying attention, or the climber drafted a novice who didn't know what he was supposed to do. The result is the same: the belayer fails to catch the fall, and both he and the climber discover whole new worlds of pain. Belaying is not a mysterious process, yet not a month goes by that I don't catch an airborne belayer before he smacks face-first into the rock or the falling climber.

Some simple principles for the belayer:

• Face the climber and pay attention.

• Take in only as much rope as the climber needs; don't keep it so taut that you involve him in a tug-of-war. (When you're belaying the leader, you'll be paying out rope, but the same principle applies.)

• Stay directly under the climber so that you won't be pulled sideways by a fall.

• Plant your foot forward on the side opposite your brake hand. If the climber substantially outweighs you, stand right up against the cliff, weak side foot braced for impact.

• Anchor yourself and use a belay device if you have any doubt about your ability to hold his fall.

Anchored, a child can hold a top-rope fall. If the stance is precarious, even a linebacker should be anchored. At Great Falls, Virginia, for example, the river is only a few feet away, and the

Syl is contemplating an overhang. Mike is belaying, securely braced, directly under the anchor. Note that alternatives to Lycra include Rugby shirt and painter's pants.

stances are small. Watching a belayer fly off a ledge and land in the Potomac can be the high point of your day. In summer the guy just gets an enviable cooling off, but in winter it would be a long, cold walk out, and in spring floods, he could drown.

In the days of canvas shorts, the body belay was used almost exclusively: it was less fuss, and if the double seats of everybody's shorts soon hung in tatters from rope friction, well, that was part of the cachet. Nylon running shorts and Lycra tights, on the other hand, can produce burns that are very painful, not to mention awkward to explain to nonclimbers. Whenever shorts that expose a little cheek are in fashion, the casualty rate goes up.

Belay devices can preserve your wardrobe and strength, but none are automatic: your responsibilities remain the same.

Clear communication is essential. The climber will ask, "On belay?" before he begins to climb. This is your signal to wake up. When both eyes are open, you reply, "Belay on," indicating that you are prepared to manage the rope and catch a fall. The climber acknowledges by saying, "Climbing," letting you know that he is no longer fussing with his shoes or performing any number of other preclimb rituals.

The climber may call, "Slack!" if he wants more rope let out; "Up rope!" if you should take it in. "Tension!" is the signal that you should take in rope until you can feel tension and hold it firmly at that point. When the climber completes the route (or, in lead climbing, has anchored himself at the next belay stance), he calls, "Off belay!" You first release the rope, then reply, "Belay off!"

Other calls may be used, depending on the nature of the partnership, audience, or inspiration.

If a hold breaks, or the climber drops a piece of gear, he will yell, "Rock!" so that those below can take cover. While teaching climbers at Seneca Rocks, West Virginia, I once encountered another party that included a climber named Rock. After the second time someone shouted to him, I was able to persuade them to call him by his last name.

The formal calls can become important on a crag when distance, noise, and wind make communication difficult. For top roping it can be pretty casual, but it is still essential for the climber to assure himself that you, the belayer, are doing your job. Granted, in an intense social scene, this can be difficult. You may be a lot more interested in looking at someone else or, after you have gained experience, edifying a fresh audience with your latest climbing epic, related in fascinating detail. Such preoccupations can be unnerving to your partner, especially if he is grappling with difficult moves. He may start to ask nervous questions, like "Have you got me?" — a polite way of telling you to shut up, control your hormones, and watch *his* ass. Male climbers can get into trouble with testosterone.

It is also smart not to belay or climb if there are any traces of foreign substances, legal or controlled, swimming around in your blood. When climbing stoned was popular, summit registers used to contain entries from groups like the Cannabis Climbers' Club. Dope seems to have dropped off, along with some of its aficionados. Actually, despite their inevitable motto ("We climb higher"), these guys never got high enough to fall very far — for one thing, carrying a couple of pounds of Oreos impeded progress — and they spent most of their time sitting on ledges, enjoying the view. If you're serious about climbing, though, just say LATER.

Deus ex machina

The deal among climbers is that if you can competently belay someone, you get your turn at climbing. But remember, you are responsible for your own safety. Know that a major hazard in top roping is the bozo anchor, guaranteed to scare the living daylights out of you. It's just not a good idea to climb on a rig without knowing exactly what's up top, and you can't see the whole works from below. Everybody climbs with strangers sooner or later. Don't be shy about looking over their anchor or asking the rope's owner what you are tying yourself into; it's not considered impolite. And don't make assumptions. Just because someone looks like a fairly competent climber doesn't mean he always knows what he is doing. One of the best climbers I've ever known always rigged a top rope with a couple of half hitches — fine if you're hitching a mule, but not real secure. I gave up nagging him about it, but I always watched. All it would have taken to loosen those hitches was somebody bumping into the rope. I chose to climb with him anyway, but as your mother used to tell you, do as I say, not as I do.

To set yourself up for top roping, you tie an anchor (usually

11mm static rope like the stuff cavers use, made by Bluewater or PMI) to a stout tree or boulder atop the cliff. Tie a loop in the other end, clip in two carabiners, and clip in the midpoint of the climbing rope. The carabiner gates should be reversed or opposed or both, so that the gates cannot open simultaneously. The loop in the anchor rope can be made with a figure-eight knot on a bight, or loop, followed up with an overhand to secure the working end of the rope. To tie the other end of the anchor, use a bowline — it's the easiest knot to work with. The photo shows the result. (We will go over all the knots in detail in the next chapter; they're not complicated or hard to learn.)

Hang the anchor rope just over the edge of the cliff and throw down the ends of the climbing rope. If there are people around, first yell, "Rope!" to warn them that 8 pounds of nylon is coming down. They may reply, "Clear!" if everything is okay, or any of various expletives if someone is bouldering right below.

Some climbers use 1-inch webbing as a top-rope anchor. In a very secure situation, this might be okay, if you can be quite certain the anchor won't move over any sharp edges. The webbing is plenty strong enough, but it cuts more easily than rope. Put it under tension holding a climber, or saw it back and forth catching the weight of a falling climber, and you definitely have a prescription for disaster.

Don't underestimate what friction can do to even the best equipment. I once rigged a familiar climb, using 11mm Bluewater rope. This is heavy-duty rope, it didn't run over any sharp edges, it wouldn't move around catching a fall — everything looked good. Two friends borrowed my rig to do a variation on this climb and flipped the anchor over a little so that it was straight over their route. After falling many times on this hard climb, they flipped the rope back, and I started up the original route. As I reached the crux, about halfway up, a tourist stuck his head over the top of the cliff and said, "Say, did you know that your rope's cut?" I was real impressed with the possibilities. After a few deep breaths, I gingerly moved through the crux, finished the climb, and took a look. The sheath had sawn through on a small quartz nubbin over where the rope had served for the variation. The core would have held a top-rope fall . . . maybe. Now I slide some old 1-inch runners over the 11mm rope, moving them to points of friction. I have never had to replace any of the webbing or buy a new anchor rope, but I feel better about what's holding me, and that's what counts.

Lead climbing

Leading the way, reading the rock, confidently placing the protection, using all your skills in seemingly effortless combination, with nothing but the sky above you: yes, this is lead climbing. But it's best to learn how to lead by following somebody who already knows. It is, after all, more risky: should the second fall, he is almost immediately caught by the rope, but the leader would fall twice the distance to his last protection, plus some rope stretch.

Start in a party of three. You, as the least experienced climber, can come up second, unclipping each piece of protection, then clipping it into another rope, which you are trailing for the third climber. (A threesome would be very awkward with only one rope, since pitches couldn't be longer than about 65 feet.) The third climber removes the protection.

Clipping through the protection in a party of three — without having to either place the anchors or remove them — allows you to concentrate on the climbing and deal with the exposure, which can be unnerving on your first few pitches. Suddenly you see nothing but air under your feet, and you realize that if you screw up, you could fall farther than you ever even thought about. Don't underestimate the power of this new experience. Even if you are a good top-rope climber, you may have trouble following your first few pitches. There is a lot more going on, both mentally and physically, and some of the moves are not familiar. Easy leads usually follow cracks for good protection. A top roper accustomed to delicate face moves may get lost working a corner, or dihedral. Using both walls of the corner comes naturally to some people, but it could be a new concept. Don't be surprised, or embarrassed: many talented face climbers, people with real gymnastic ability, fall when trying their first dihedral.

After a few pitches of playing the middleman, you'll want to try your hand at seconding. Now you're responsible for belaying the leader and removing the protection. It helps a lot if you first play around with the hardware while standing on nice solid ground. Practice placing and removing the metal anchors, or chocks, before you have to do it while hanging on with one hand. Become familiar with the techniques of carrying and arranging all the hardware. Leaders are very fussy about their racks of equipment; they really do need to know where everything is. It saves a lot of time if you can rack it in the right order, and you are less likely to get yourself all tangled up in the gear.

Handling the gear for yourself will tell you which types of hardware you prefer. If possible, use your partner's rack a few times before buying your own.

Getting in gear

To start, you don't have to invest in a lot of expensive equipment — all you really need is the desire to climb.

Some crags are pretty hard on beginners. Nice rough granite gives hiking boots and sneakers something to grab, but polished schist or sandstone can be very frustrating without climbing shoes. Still, there is a lot to be said for sneakers and boots. For one thing, getting to climbs often requires scrambling in just such footwear. Walking is the thing climbing shoes are worst for; they cost too much to be worn out just walking around.

For another, boots are a necessity in mountaineering and winter climbing. Maybe you don't plan on this type of climbing, but if it's a possibility, you would do well to put in some time on rock wearing boots.

Third, climbing shoes make you dependent on them and can actually limit your growth as a climber. Sure, they make you look good fast, but your technique ends up based far too much on friction, on using the smooth, sticky rubber of the climbing shoe. Learning *edging* — using the stiff edge of a boot to stay in balance — is a little less natural. In lead climbing, edging is important because it allows you to stand in balance and look over moves or place protection. You won't make as much progress right away in hiking boots, but you'll eventually go further.

Finally, today's climbing shoes have soles so soft that they last only a little while. As a beginner, you're just going to chew them up. You'll scrape at the rock with your feet, and each sliding fall will tear away rubber. I watched someone destroy a pair of the latest hundred-dollar hot shoes in three weekends. Why not beat up on something cheaper? It takes a lot of abuse to destroy a lug sole. Yes, you will want good climbing shoes, but just don't be in too much of a rush.

At some point you will want a rope. If you are doing a lot of top roping, buy the cheapest one you can get, since top roping is hard on rope: it wears down quickly, loses its waterproof treatment, and starts to get kinky. These bad handling qualities can get pretty scary if you use the rope for leading, which is complicated enough without an uncooperative rope. Reserve your cheap rope for top roping, where handling qualities don't matter. In fact, a rope that should be retired for leading can still be used for top roping almost indefinitely as long as the sheath is not cut or worn through. But buy a used rope only from a climber you know and trust. You should offer no more than half the cost of an inexpensive new rope.

Ropes come in lengths of 150 and 165 feet (45 and 50 meters). Since today's ropes are light, weight is not much of a factor, and most people therefore use the 165-foot length. As a beginner, you'll probably feel more comfortable with a single 10–11mm rope than a pair of double 8–9mm ropes: learning to handle one rope properly is complicated enough.

What other gear you want to buy depends on what kind of climbing you will be doing, and how good you look in Lycra. You can top-rope forever with shoes, a chalk bag, a rope and anchor, and two carabiners. If you buy a commercially sewn climbing harness, buy a belay device: a butt belay, with the rope running right over the leg loops, will make your new harness untrustworthy for holding a leader fall almost immediately. Money down the drain.

Elements of style

There are some conventions about how to describe the style of an ascent. A *traditional* ascent of a pitch means climbing it in one go, no top roping or rappelling to rehearse. If you do it without first watching others climb the pitch, you make an *on-sight* ascent. Getting up without first asking other climbers to describe the sequence of moves (*Beta,* like the video) would give you a *flash* of the route.

If you fall during a traditional ascent, you lower yourself to the belay or to the ground, and pull the rope down. You could reclimb the first section, clipping into the protection, then finish the route. If you lower yourself but don't pull the rope down, it's called a *yo-yo*, and if you hang on the rope where you fell, you are *hangdogging*.

Ethics and other crimes

In the beginning the leader ventured into the unknown. Today, some climbers first inspect a climb on rappel, or top-rope it before attempting a lead. But the real decline, if not fall, of ethics started with the practice of gardening, or cleaning unclimbed rock. First it was cleaning dirt and loose stones out of cracks to make room for protection. The leader used to do it with a curved-pick climbing hammer, a nut tool, or a long piton. Not surprisingly, seconds objected to the shower of dirt and rocks, so some climbers started cleaning on rappel. They extended gardening to removing loose flakes, and then to scraping away lichen with a wire brush.

After gardening came fixed protection. Since the climber was hanging around cleaning the route, why not put in protection where it would be problematic? Pitons were hammered into cracks too narrow for the chocks of the time. Nut placement was difficult in horizontal cracks, too, but a pin could be totally safe — bombproof. So the pin was placed and left in, rather than retrieved and replaced each time with consequent damage to the rock.

It was the first compromise, the first break in the notion that you placed protection as you climbed, climbed without protection, or didn't climb. The fixed pin was done for the best of reasons, to protect the rock from repeated nailing, but it turned out to be the first step in the process of guaranteeing a climber's ability to do a climb. Doubt about the outcome of a climb could be lessened, if not removed altogether. Since doubt may be the only thing a climber really conquers, its absence, for some, killed the sport.

As nuts improved, climbers began to fix nuts, too. There was little argument for these. They were put in where you simply could not stop to place protection. They were an admission that you couldn't climb some routes in the old style. It was not much of a step from fixed nuts to bolts.

Bolts were placed where there were no cracks to allow protection. The bolt opened up blank faces, whole new worlds to climb. At first bolts were placed on the lead, but this was difficult and dangerous. Tenuous stances often produced untrustworthy bolts, and a bad bolt was worse than no bolt at all. It seemed ethically preferable to place a safe bolt, like a fixed pin, on rappel. Some traditionalists tried using skyhooks, tiny hooks used for aid on nubbins or flakes, as an alternative to bolting on rappel. Hooking could be a little safer than placing on the lead, but not much. All you had to do was sneeze and you were going for the ride.

So rappel-placed bolts began to appear. Those who drilled holes while clinging to precarious holds or hanging from their ropes prayed for the invention of a lightweight, powerful, workable power drill. For a decade our ethics were protected by engineering problems. But driven by the construction industry, engineers solved the problems, the power drill arrived, and ethics crumbled.

In Europe now they chisel holds into blank faces and paint lines to mark the routes. The latest in America? Sawing down trees to let sunlight dry the cliffs.

Style is a regional issue. A California climber visiting Carderock once asked me, "Where are the bolts?" I explained that they were unacceptable to the climbers, and besides, we were in a national park. He was surprised at our self-restraint. In California, he said, no amount of intimidation can stop the punks from putting in rappel-placed bolts to claim new lead climbs.

Some practices acceptable in one area are not acceptable in another. The only rule is to accept what the local climbers have agreed upon.

How hard is it?

Climbs are rated for their degree of commitment and technical difficulty. There are numerous grading systems: British, French, Alpine, Australian, American. The most widely used system on this side of the Atlantic is as follows:

Commitment

I   A couple of hours
II   Half a day
III Most of a day
IV A long day, perhaps more
V   More than one day, more than two for slower parties or poor conditions
VI More than two days, and serious, if not downright nuts

Technical difficulty

1   Walking
2   Scrambling, using hands occasionally
3   Climbing, using hands
4   Difficult or exposed enough to rope up and belay
5   Difficult enough to require intermediate points of protection between belays
5.0   Easy, in the scheme of things
5.1
5.2
5.3
5.4   Protection becomes very important
5.5
5.6
5.7   Usually requires well-developed climbing skills and protection abilities
5.8   A competent weekend climber may find some moves strenuous or technically complex
5.9   Difficult, period
5.10a Meaningfully difficult
    b
    c
    d
5.11a Imaginary holds
    b
    c
    d

5.12a   Imaginary climbs
   b
   c
   d
5.13a   Not for mere mortals
   b
   c
   d

The letter subgrades for technical difficulty reflect the fact that as the numbers go up, the area of difficulty keeps getting larger. It's hard to tell a 5.2 from a 5.1, for example, but a 5.11 is very different from a 5.10.

Experience, training, natural ability, and attitude determine at what level a climber can competently perform. Some climbs are size specific, easier for short or tall people, or for small or large hands. If you aren't the right size, these climbs can be several grades harder. For weekend climbers, anything they get caught doing below 5.7 is "classic," 5.7 to 5.8 is "interesting," 5.9 is "hard," and routes 5.10 and above are grounds for any number of outrageous lies.

Do the numbers really mean anything? Well, yes and no. Standards up to 5.9 can vary wildly throughout North America. Routes of 5.9 and above, if they were rated before the mid-'70s, were the work of a small number of people who did one another's climbs and graded consistently throughout their region. Eastern climbs tended to be harder for their grade than Colorado climbs, and Yosemite climbs were easier still. Climbers in some areas were reluctant to introduce 5.10, since it violated the original decimal system; 5.9s in such places may be very tricky, if not actually death routes, unless they have been upgraded by consensus. In New Hampshire, for example, any climb in the guidebook with a + grade is likely to be very gripping. Newer climbs have been rated by climbers who have traveled to many areas and been exposed to broader views of what constitutes difficulty.

There are other factors, too. A 5.9 crack climb in Yosemite might seem easy to a 5.9 leader used to crack techniques. To an eastern climber, more adept at face techniques, that same crack is desperate. To a Yosemite climber, Seneca Rocks can seem terrifyingly steep. A Gunkie finds Seneca's vertical cracks hard to protect, while a Seneca climber gets uneasy protecting the horizontal cracks of the Shawangunks. Devil's Tower is the crack climber's paradise; the nearby Needles, in the Black Hills of South Dakota, may be the ultimate in face climbing.

Since climbs have these numbers, folks are bound to keep score. People do compete in climbing. Just remember that competition is not always healthy. If you fudge about how you did a climb, someone may be inspired to try it in the style you claimed. Placing protection and working out moves without rehearsal or sneak previews require reserves of strength, skill, and nerve. You aren't responsible if others are kidding themselves, if they can't admit their own limitations, or worse, if they can't abide someone else's abilities, but people can get physically injured if you lead them on.

Choosing your partner

Just as you have to be careful about describing your exploits, you need to be sure of your climbing partners' skills and veracity. As in any sport, there are a number of so-called participants who talk a better game than they play. No one is spared their epic tales and sage advice. Large amounts of alcohol may serve as a lubricant for the producers, but no amount can anesthetize their victims. Someday one of these people may corner you at a climbing area or, more likely, a climbing equipment store, which they haunt day and night, tormenting the staff, making them atone for their crass commercialism and enviable discount.

When confronted with this crashing bore, take the offensive. He will be more offensive, but your only hope is to persuade him to find another victim, preferably one out of earshot. Start out with, "Haven't seen you climbing lately." His response begins with a long, drawn-out "Well . . ." followed by the opening excuse. Until the Fourth of July in the Northern Hemisphere, he'll say, "It's too early in the season." After that it's too hot. By October, it's too cold.

Sometimes this excuse is accompanied by a confession that he's not yet in top form. Of course, he owns a rowing machine, climbing simulator, and finger board, and he belongs to two health clubs, one near the office, the other near home. He never gets to climb because he has a permanent case of tendinitis from working out. He compares dosages of Motrin and always wins.

Another ploy is that he's developing a new area. "I've been working some *desperate* stuff on this cliff I've found," he'll say. Remarkable that nobody else has ever climbed there.

If he lives near an East Coast crag, he fancies himself a mountaineer. The Seattle bore must claim to be a rock jock. Coloradans face the problem of having it all, which makes it fun to watch them weasel. The bore who knows no shame will claim to have soloed everything. This is a bit risky, since it leaves him open to challenge, but the true 12-gauge bore can dismiss this with a contemptuous retort: "Who would follow me if I lead it? Might as well solo."

By definition, bores own all the latest gear and can harangue unsuspecting beginners for hours with lectures on the merits of their choice of equipment. They know the weight in grams of every carabiner ever made and the precise size range of the most obscure nuts. Since they don't climb, they have lots of time to agonize over gear for the perfect hypothetical ascent.

The point is, don't get suckered into actually climbing with one of these guys. At any given time there are an astonishing number of climbers who are kidding themselves. It's just like everything else in life, only you find out the bad news while risking life and limb.

As a general rule, avoid anyone who learned to climb in the military, is involved in mountain rescue, or still carries a piton hammer. Military climbing accepts casualties, mountain rescue is for guys who need an excuse to get out of cutting the grass, and piton hammers went out with the dinosaurs. As with all rules, however, the exceptions prove it true. I have done some of my most enjoyable climbing with people who fall into one or more of those categories.

The conventional wisdom holds that climbing with your partner in a romantic relationship is a prescription for disaster, exceeded only by climbing with a *possible* lover. It can be difficult for a lot of couples, and it just may not be smart for some, but such situations have provided me with the climbing days I will always remember. It's probably a mistake, but if I'm lucky, I'll continue to do it.

2

SKILLS

The force you work against here is gravity, something you probably take for granted since it has been working on you in much the same way since you took your first step. Once you start to climb, however, you really feel its pull, and surprise, it gets more complicated than remembering where the center of the earth is. Your body's apparent weight must be overcome by the force of muscular exertion and the knack of positioning its mass. You position the body's mass by balance and by simply wedging it between such objects as rock walls or the sides of a crack. Get mass, or dead weight if you like, to do the work, and don't rely on muscular exertion. Your muscles will tire anyway, but your bones will stay the same shape.

Balance is tricky stuff. We all admire the routine of a gymnast on a balance beam, yet the balance beam is at least ten times wider than the largest hold on a moderate climb. You have to learn balance, play with it, even fall off trying to push the limits. Make the least muscular effort pay off by pushing right to the edge of balance. Gravity is going to play with you soon enough, so learn to play with it. When you've positioned yourself in perfect balance, the effort required to maintain position is minimal, and that is the name of the game. Make the easy things come easy; it will get hard soon.

The fundamentals

So there are several simple principles for efficient climbing. Use techniques that employ the body's mass, balance, strength. Keep hands and heels low — about head height for handholds, heels parallel or lower than toes. Maintain three points of contact with the rock. Keep moves static rather than dynamic (avoid lunging). Always mentally work out moves before trying them; know where you are going and how you can get there. A little mental effort can save a lot of physical strain.

All of those principles are violated on every climb, but the climber who violates them least climbs with the greatest efficiency. Efficiency saves strength, the one thing that every climber will run out of sooner or later.

Mass — whether you have more or less of it, the idea is to put it in the right place. Jam a fist in a crack, bridge across a gap with your legs, do whatever it takes.

In a jam

To work, jams need not be bloody, painful, and desperate, though sometimes they are and sometimes your fear makes you dig in for dear life. Look at a jam crack the same way you would place protection. Choose a big place over a small place. Insert body part, pull down until stuck and crank on it. (Now you know what the banding on the side of your climbing shoe is for.) Some sideways camming often makes the fit more secure. You can tape your hands to mimic the rubber banding; it doesn't work as well but it beats tearing off hunks of flesh. Applying tincture of benzoin or Tuff-skin as a taping base will help a lot. Use a cloth athletic tape, like Cramer's or Johnson & Johnson Zonas.

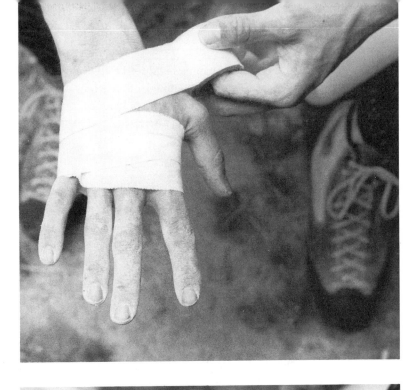

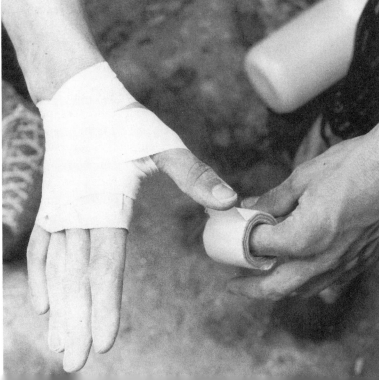

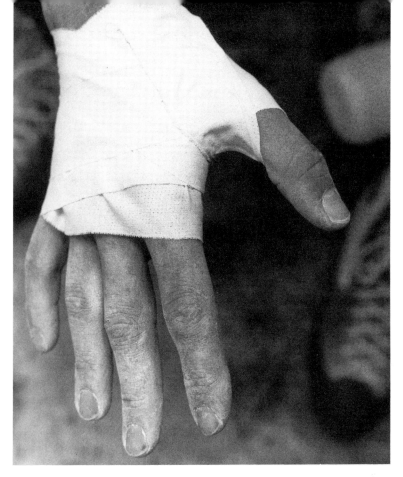

Taping up. Start on the outside of the hand at the knuckles. Pull the tape off the roll, then press it against your hand (don't wrap your hand under tension from the roll—it will be way too tight). Go across the knuckles, then the palm, then across the back of the hand with a slight overlap of the previous wrap. Eastern climbers tend to make do with a third wrap that goes down under the thumb and ends at the inside of the wrist. Western crack climbers do extra wraps for complete coverage; they anchor the tape with a complete circuit of the wrist, then go over the back of the hand and above the thumb, to finish on the palm. Some do still another wrap around the thumb. You can even make a tape glove, starting with foam prewrap, and using tape loops over the thumb and little finger. The glove is closed with a piece of tape on the inside of the wrist; cutting just this piece after each use saves on tape for the low-budget climber.

SKILLS   23

The idea is to start big and work your way down until something sticks. Jamming a whole foot is better than stacking a couple of fingers. But don't be afraid to break the rules. I was leading a classic climb on Devil's Tower when I had to wait for a party of four above to do the crux pitch. Each climber was totally out of control, struggling with a big crack. When my turn came, I knew I had to find something easier. I found a nice hand-sized crack, providing safe, secure jams and protection placements, hidden in the wall of the larger crack. The crux was no problem.

For a hand jam, first think about your feet. Where are you going to stand? This has more to do with how you can jam a crack than anything you do with your hands. Can you stem across a dihedral and face into the crack at the back, to jam it, or do you have to layback? Jams usually occur in sequence, so think about which hand or foot you want to start with, and visualize where you are going to go from there. You can shuffle hands and feet, keeping them in the same order, or you can walk them up the crack, moving each higher in turn, left passing above right, or vice versa.

Liebacking (laybacking, whatever). Pull with the arms, elbows locked. The feet could be placed flat on the right hand wall. Laybacking is strenuous, and committing — if a foot or hand slips, you're gone.

Hand jam with the thumb up. The thumb is outside the crack since the fingers fit the slot nicely.

Jams are not something that you want to reach very high to place — they work best at head height or below. Though you can't place them high, you can move quite high on them. A hand jam can be very good even though you have moved up so that it is well below your waist.

You may need to lean left to get weight over a left hand or foot jam, and do the opposite for a right jam. The weight of the upper body can make the jam more secure and provide a little rotation against the sides of the crack.

For hand jams, you choose whether to jam thumb up or thumb down, whichever feels better. You may often find that one hand positioned each way will give you good balance over the crack. The hand jam can be enlarged by sliding the thumb across the palm. You are using the meat of your hand, below your thumb, rather than the palm.

Finger jams can also be done thumb up or down. As the crack widens, the fingers can be stacked to double the size of the jam.

Hand jam with the thumb down. The thumb presses on the side of the crack in opposition to the fingers.

More jams. TOP, thumb down. BOTTOM, thumb up. The thumbs lie across the palm in this wide crack. When your hands are up high, you are mostly pulling down; as you move up, you can often pull slightly outward.

Finger jams can be excruciating, however, and tape doesn't work as well on fingers as it does on your whole hand. It is harder to get the tape well anchored on your finger without cutting off circulation. If the crack is deep enough to get more than one joint in, you can flex the fingers to increase the size range of the jam. Fingertip jams work a lot better than they look.

Obviously, size is a big deal for jams. Small hands and feet can make desperately thin cracks a breeze, while ordinary fist-sized cracks become off-width nightmares. It is worth noting that you may need to pick your shoes to accommodate the types of crack you are most likely to encounter, since the toe shapes and thicknesses may determine what you can do. A very trim shoe can be jammed across the ball of the foot, while a beefier boot will fit only if it's turned vertically, with the sole parallel to the crack. (Now you know what the little rubber toe cap is for.)

Bridging is jamming with your whole body. Climbers usually think of bridging as something done with their feet, but opposing

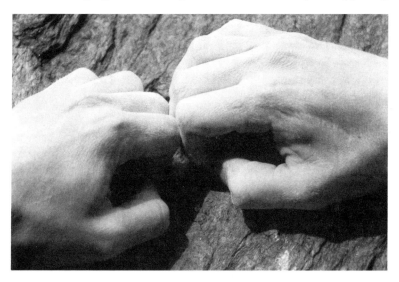

Opposition. Opposing force can hold you up. Obviously, letting go to move your hands up is tricky. Place your feet carefully on the best holds you can find to keep your balance, scope out the next handhold, and move quickly.

handholds can work to support body weight while you move your feet. You wouldn't want to spend a lot of time in this position, but it can be a very efficient technique to make quick progress.

Hold on

Handholds and footholds both come in two types: friction and edges. A friction handhold may sound rather tenuous, but if you have two other secure holds, it can provide the added stability you need to make a strenuous move. Palming a hold is the best example. You get friction with the palm to negate torque, or to briefly support weight. You may not have the satisfying grip of a well-defined edge, but the hold can be effective and less strenuous.

Handholds with edges come in a variety of shapes and sizes. The main characteristic of shape is whether you can get the fingers entirely around the hold. A flake and the classic jug (from jug handle) are the best examples. The fingers exert an outward force that locks the hold into the palm; these are the most secure of handholds, and the most intuitive.

The size of a handhold determines how many fingers you can get on it, and how much of each finger. If you can bend the fingers and get two joints in contact, the hold is more stable and less strenuous than if you have to rely on just one joint. Getting fingertips horizontally on a hold may be more secure but can be strenuous. Try to hang on with the fingertips vertical, coming down on the hold. The base of the hand, near the wrist, can act as a fulcrum for the fingers. You are forming a triangle of support, rather than quivering on your tips.

The important fingers to get on a hold are the index and middle fingers. The thumb and index finger are your strongest, so you can use the thumb on the side of a hold, or slip it on top of your fingers on a hold. The ring finger and little finger are less useful on their own, but they can greatly improve strength and stability. Even if you can't make contact on the hold with the outside fingers, they broaden the base of your strength if you tuck them alongside, mimicking the action of the fingers that are in contact. The muscles across the palm and the outside of the hand are lending support.

Remember that holds come in two directions: up and down. You can undercling even the tiniest edges. Don't think of the undercling as restricted to big cracks or obvious flakes.

A friction foothold is often used with the toes straight in. The toes flex at the ball of the foot, giving maximum contact of the sole and maximum leverage from the foot. The pressure into the rock causes adhesion and your foot sticks, supporting your weight. The more surface contact, the safer the hold. A bigger hold allows you to move higher, or to shift the upper body to improve balance. Small holds require you to concentrate on remaining as still as possible, to avoid the slightest shift of the foot and loss of adhesion. You often feel like you can't take your eyes off your foot, or you'll fall.

Corners and bulges can allow you to use friction with a greater area of the foot. You may use the ball of the foot, as you would on an edge, with the toes pointing to the sides. Drop the heel to keep maximum contact with the rock; that will also rest your calf muscles.

Edging can be done with the ball of the foot or with the toe. Again, keep the heel low, and think about positioning your upper body to force your feet *into* the rock. The upper body must be *away* from the rock to press your feet in. Really *look* at the edge you are going to use. Look for the angle of the hold, and for any irregularities that decrease the usable surface area or make the hold unstable. Match the profile of the hold with the angle of your foot. If you are using the ball of the foot, with the toe pointing out, you may have to angle the toe upward or down to match the hold.

The importance of studying the rock cannot be stressed too much. Just as you plan moves, routes, and chock placements, you must study individual holds to get the best results. This may be a slow process at first, but you will get better with practice, and it will become almost instinctual. Soon you will cease to be aware of the effort, and the moves will flow from your mind to your limbs.

Special cases

Mantle. The mantleshelf, or simply mantle, is a technique unto itself. You place your hands on holds or a ledge, as wide as possible, and pull down. As the hands pass your chest level, you press down

Undercling. Holds come in lots of directions. By pressing with the feet and pulling up with the hands, you remain upright. Notice that the heels are kept low, and the upper body is out from the rock to transmit most of the force to the legs.

The mantle, or mantleshelf move, is not as awkward as it looks. Hands are spread wide apart. Feet can either be placed between the hands, or as seen here. Then you stand up. It's mostly a matter of balance and belief.

and keep going until you can place your feet between your hands. Then stand up. You can practice on the side of a staircase, or a flat-topped retaining wall.

Offwidth. Offwidth techniques are a mixture of crack climbing and face climbing, with a lot of stress and strain built in. One arm and leg get inside the crack and work around for holds or counter-pressure to hold up the body. The limbs outside the crack can do most of the lifting, then the inside limbs repeat the process to gain stability higher up. It can be a real struggle.

Offwidth. The idea is to use arm–shoulder and foot–leg combinations to press on opposite sides of the crack. It is more strenuous than jamming and less secure.

Chimney. If the crack widens up a bit, you have a squeeze chimney, which is about as attractive as it sounds. You place a hand and a foot on each side of the crack, or both hands on one side and both feet on the other, and press to lever your way upward. The hardest thing about a squeeze chimney is seeing what you're doing. You often have to enter the chimney with your head turned to the side, and you may not be able to turn it once inside. To do one such pitch, I had to take off my helmet and clip it to my harness, so that it hung outside the crack. Everything went fine until my empty hammer holster, recently used for an ice tool, got hung up on something. There was nothing to do but unbuckle the holster and carry it up in my teeth.

Your own size can make a big difference in a squeeze chimney. To follow one pitch, I simply walked to the back of the crack and climbed the staircase of rock inside. The leader, a big guy, hadn't fit in there and had struggled with the pitch; he was not happy when he saw the rope snaking inside the crack.

By the same token, small stature can be a terminal disadvantage in a wide chimney. When the walls are too far apart for you to reach, you pick one and start face climbing. You get an uncomfortable feeling knowing the other wall is looming behind you, ready to bounce you around like a pinball if you fall.

Traversing

Climbing up may be the goal, but you will spend a good deal of time climbing from side to side. Traversing can also be a form of training. Bouldering sideways, a few feet off the ground, can give you the maximum workout in the minimum time. Traversing makes you more aware of shifting your weight in order to make a move. You can move farther to the right if your left toe is pointing left. Think in terms of pulling and pushing with your hands.

Carefully switching from one hand or foot to the other on the same hold is a skill that comes with practice. It can get you over the thin spots. You can even hop quickly from one foot to the other when the hold is just too small to accommodate even a tiny bit of each shoe. If you lean out on your arms, you can step through on your footholds, rather than shuffle your feet every time. You have to face sideways and use the outside edge of your trailing foot, but it is a quick way to cover ground if the moves are easy enough. Don't scrape at holds with your feet.

Newtonian climbing

Try to develop a rhythm to keep you moving. Don't hesitate in midmove, especially if you are climbing upward, because you will lose momentum and start fighting gravity, rather than flow along.

The laws of physics dictate this. Objects in motion tend to stay in motion; those at rest tend to stay at rest. It's easier to move when you are moving — there is a certain lightness to pulling upward when you have already pushed up with your feet.

You are weightless when you reach the apogee of each move. It is easier to move hands or feet at that point because you don't have to support your weight. Miss it by a millisecond and it can be crash and burn, but hit that sweet spot and you are flying. The Germans, who study everything to death, call this the "Toter Punkt." That sounds like a rock group with Mohawk haircuts, but it means the dead point, and it neatly describes the moment at which you can move with the minimum of effort.

The same principle has to be applied to all muscular effort. You want to position yourself so that the least effort will sustain you. Think in terms of your center of gravity, and the direction that gravity is pulling on you. Shift your weight to maximize your balance and let your bone structure carry most of the load. It requires far less effort to support yourself from an arm that's fully extended, with elbow locked, than from one bent at the elbow, with the muscles flexing. Hang from bone, which is durable stuff, not muscle and tendon — those things wear out.

What you do with the unweighted limb, or limbs, while making a move can spell success or crash. Work the unweighted limb like a counterweight, to aid your balance or increase the velocity of your movement. This takes a while to learn, but start by always trying to remember what effect each limb will have on your position. Don't let a dangling foot keep you from reaching the crux handhold. Think about getting it to do something for you even if you don't have a hold for it.

When the muscles weaken and begin to twitch from exertion and tension, unweight each limb in turn and shake it out, allowing the muscles to relax. Hyperventilating can help to clear this up a bit and will also clear the head, allowing you to concentrate on the problem at hand. The popularity of the chalk bag can be understood if you consider chalking a way of resting the small muscles of the hand. Such rests are the key to climbing in control.

Anchors away

Learning how to attach yourself to an anchor is a crucial skill. This may sound a bit strange, but a good number of climbers often don't know what (if anything) they are clipped into. I recall one climber who was cautioned by his partner not to lean back on his anchor, as it consisted of a knotted sling jammed into a crack. They were on a small, crowded ledge in the dark, so this was not comforting information.

Anchors will be discussed in detail later, but the point to be stressed here is that you should know exactly what is attaching you to the rock and how it will work in case of a fall. You should have no doubt in your mind that you are clipped into something substantial: a runner of sufficient strength with screwgate carabiners throughout the chain, or two standard carabiners with the gates reversed and opposed. To properly arrange two standard carabiners, clip them in together, then rotate one 180 degrees. In this position, the gates cannot both be inadvertently opened. Be aware that round screw

Carabiners, gates reversed and opposed. These are a couple of lightweights, high praise for a carabiner. They are Ds made by Chouinard and Omega.

collars on locking carabiners can be rotated by friction on rope, rock, or the human backside, and thus be opened.

The crucial point is to make sure that no link in the anchor chain can fail. Any competent climber who is seconding must be able to securely attach himself to the anchor system and should have the gear available to do so. Chances are that the leader is already carrying a bewildering assortment of equipment; he should not have to carry more for the exclusive use of his second. If you're leading, make sure the belayer has what he needs. This may sound trivial, but the temptation is strong for experienced climbers to rush through setting up the belay because the upcoming lead is foremost in their minds. They commit to the climb, then engage in a shouting match with the ill-prepared belayer. It is the responsibility of the leader to assure himself that his belayer has sufficient equipment and knowledge to conduct the belay, clean the protection, and clip in at the next stance.

As the belayer, you are using some sort of harness or waist loop to which anchors and belaying or rappelling devices can be attached. You should have several carabiners and slings of appropriate length, and you should be conversant with the body rappel and belay (described later). The reason for this is that beginners and experts alike can drop things, and the classic case is the figure 8 descender ("Gee, how do I get down without that thing?").

Knowing your knots

The fundamental skills are simple and can be mastered in a couple of hours. Much of climbing is merely the application of basics to the task at hand. Once these basics become second nature, sophisticated techniques will come more easily.

The bare minimum in knot-tying ability is the figure-eight knot, and the Prusik knot, which can be used as a safety on rappel and to tie off a fallen leader. You can climb safely with these, but it is often convenient to know more knots. Knots are tools and more knowledge gives you more flexibility. Learn the knots long before you go climbing. You can practice them at home, where there is no pressure, until you feel comfortable tying them.

ROCK SPORT

The figure-eight, or Flemish bend, is the strongest, most secure knot to tie into your harness. It is almost idiot-proof, but is 10 percent stronger if the working end *stays on the* inside *and no strands are crossed. To secure the tail, finish off with an* overhand knot *or half a double fisherman's bend. You can also use it to join two ropes of the same diameter.*

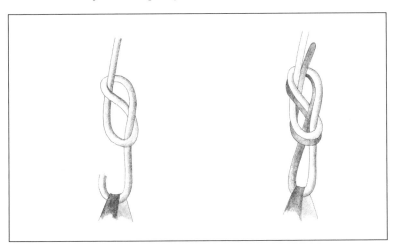

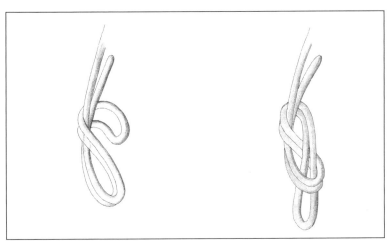

The figure-eight on a bight (loop) is quickly tied, easy to untie after it has held weight, and very strong. It's the best knot for attaching yourself to anchors.

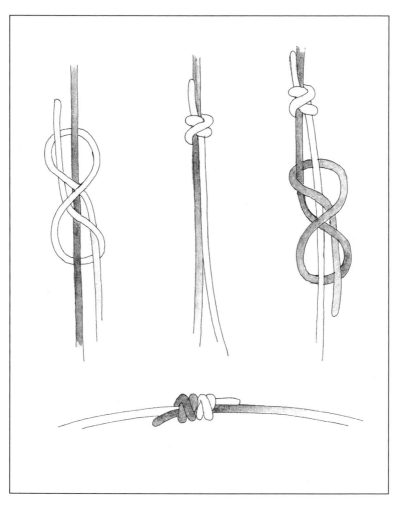

Double fisherman's knot. A useful knot for slings, or joining ropes of different diameters for a rappel. The knot is also called the Grapevine (you'll understand why when you tie it). The working end coils around the standing end twice and is fed under the coils to form half the knot. The process is repeated with the other end, and the halves are pulled together. The knot sets hard when weighted. Leave an inch or more of tail and tighten the knot firmly because the tails are pulled into the knot by impact force. Use pliers to tighten sling knots.

ROCK SPORT

Prusik, the classic ratchet knot. It will slide along a rope when loose, but tighten when weighted. It is used to ascend a fixed rope, as a self-belay while rappelling, and to secure a fallen leader. In an emergency, a small chock sling can be used as a Prusik.

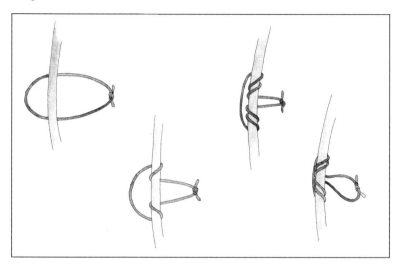

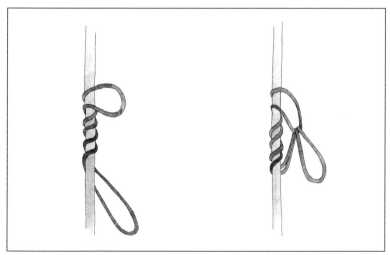

The Klemheist (Headon). This variation on the Prusik is easier to tie one-handed and works with a webbing sling.

The Bachmann. If you actually have to ascend a fixed rope, this is the most efficient knot. The carabiner makes the knot a lot easier to move. A carabiner made from rectangular stock works better than one with a round profile. Once the sling starts wrapping around the fixed rope, don't get the strands twisted. The sling provides the grip; if it slips, don't grab the carabiner harder—that will make it worse. Instead, squeeze your hand around the sling and the back of the carabiner, pulling down slightly, to get the sling to set.

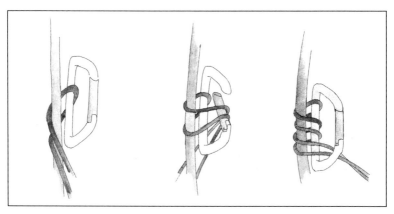

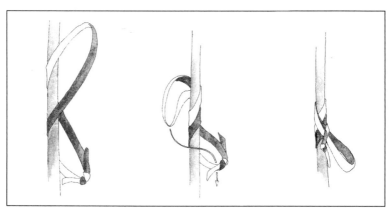

The Hedden (Kreuzklem). The simplest ratchet knot for webbing slings, it is quick and easy to tie, being a variation of the figure-eight. It is a valuable knot, since you will almost always have a webbing sling close at hand in an emergency.

40   ROCK SPORT

The bowline. This classic tie-in knot is safe, but the figure-eight is stronger and nearly foolproof. It is easy to screw up a bowline when you're tired, hurried, or stressed out. Also, the end will pull back through the knot unless it is well set and tied off. Deaths and injuries have resulted from improperly tied bowlines; there have been far fewer such incidents with the figure-eight. Still, the bowline is a very useful knot because the figure-eight is so awkward to adjust. The bowline on a coil allows you to tie into the rope without a harness, and the bowline on a bight can be very handy for tying to multiple anchor points and equalizing the load on each point.

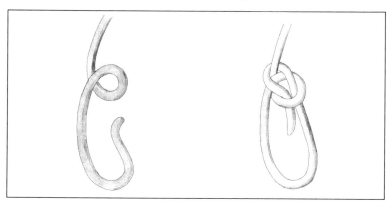

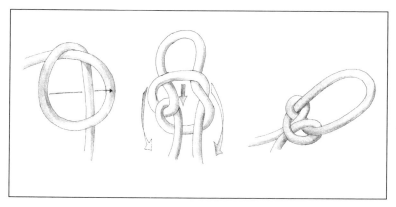

The belayer's hitch. This is a single-loop, adjustable anchor tie-in. The figure-eight is stronger and simpler but nearly impossible to adjust. Tie as shown, adjust the anchor for length, pull the top wrap down over the knot, and tighten for security.

The clove hitch, an adjustable anchor tie-in. The first loop goes on top of the second. Drop the loops over an object or clip them into a carabiner, then pull the ends to tighten. Tighten carefully inside a carabiner, or the knot will shift over onto the gate.

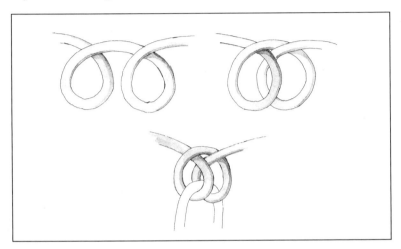

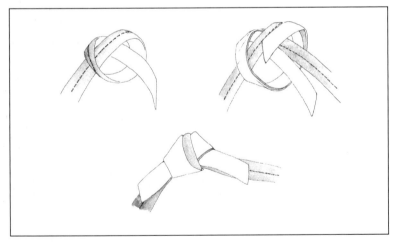

The ring bend or water knot is used to make a webbing sling. Do not use it in rope. You make an overhand knot in one end and follow back through the knot with the other end. Cinch it down tight, and leave more than an inch of tail in the ends.

ROCK SPORT

The *figure-eight* (also called a Flemish bend) is the knot of choice, as it is versatile, strong and almost idiot-proof. Even when tied wrong, it is as strong as any other knot. To tie the knot right, make sure the strands are not crossed, and that the standing end forms the outside loop. This knot can also be used to join two ropes together for a rappel, if they are roughly the same size in diameter. A figure-eight on a bight (a loop of rope) gives a strong, secure loop for clipping in, yet it's easy to loosen after it has held weight.

The figure-eight knot can be used to tie into a waist loop and form a belay without using any hardware. Simply run the rope from your tie-in around a large tree or boulder and then around the back

Jane wants to tie off this tree for a belay anchor, but she also wants to belay out at the edge of the cliff so she can watch her second climb. She loops the rope around the tree and heads back to her stance. NEXT PAGE: She then threads the rope around her harness and ties a figure-eight on a bight with an overhand safety. If she were short on rope, she could use a single strand around the tree.

of the waist loop. A bight of the rope is then tied in a figure eight, around the standing line going to the anchor. Another form of the figure-eight, the Hedden knot, can substitute for the Prusik; it will work using 1-inch tubular webbing.

To complement the figure-eight knot, I use half a double fisherman's knot to secure the ends at the tie-in. This holds better than a simple overhand. The double fisherman's knot is used for tying together ropes of different diameters for rappel, as well as for tying chock slings and runners.

Fallen leaders

The second essential among the knots is the *Prusik,* or some other ratchet knot. First, the Prusik can be used as a safety on rappels. Beginners are often wary of rappelling, and with good reason. More serious accidents occur during this maneuver than at any other single time during a day's climbing. Belaying a rappel is extremely inefficient and time-consuming. It is also downright dangerous. I don't want to spend a moment longer than I have to at a rappel point on a crowded crag. Nevertheless, it is much safer to practice rappels with a belay at the start until you are confident of your technique. The first long rappel with a little exposure will still be unnerving, but by using a Prusik you can manage it.

A fireman's belay (holding the ropes from below) does offer some security but is especially risky for the belayer. I once had a student balk at a 150-foot rappel at the end of a long day's climbing. She had practiced the rappel, but it was suddenly more than she wanted to handle. It was getting dark, so I went down the rope first, in order to belay her from below. She started out with an awkward swing and I pulled on the rope to slow her progress. Either the rope or her feet dislodged a baseball-sized rock. In the fading light I had just enough warning to spot it and decide not to move. It landed not three feet away, smashing into atoms. I gave serious consideration to finding another line of work.

The Prusik knot used in a 4-foot sling of 6mm perlon works well on 11mm rope and lasts longer than thinner rope or webbing.

If the student can absorb it, I also teach the *Klemheist* knot, which is easier to tie with one hand, and works in webbing. The *Bachmann* knot is very useful. The carabiner makes it much easier to move the knot, and it can be tied with webbing. You must remember to avoid pressure on the gate side of the carabiner and keep the load on the sling itself, not the carabiner, as the knot will slip when the carabiner is under load.

The best ascender knot for use in webbing is the *Hedden*. I think it is important to know this knot because Prusik slings may be left behind or disappear, but one can almost always locate a webbing runner.

Even if the climber does not need to belay his rappel or ascend a standing line, he must be able to tie a Prusik (or substitute) to secure a fallen lead climber. To climb with anyone who cannot do this is sheer lunacy. If the leader falls, the second must be able to get out of the belay system safely in order to render assistance. Even if the leader is not injured, he may need the second's help to get back on the climb or rig a retreat.

The idea is to first lock the leader's rope by wrapping it around your body, or tying it off above a belay device. Second, tie on a Prusik and attach it to an anchor, so that you, the second, can escape from the system. In an emergency, a small chock sling will make a good Prusik. Third, provide a more secure link to an anchor than just the Prusik. The principle is the same no matter what belay technique is used, and it is absolutely indispensable that all climbers be adept at this.

The time to learn to secure a fallen leader is when you are learning to belay. It is an integral part of belay technique, and if learned as such, it will be retained. When I teach beginners, we go through the knots, then I do a quick rappel. As the first student rappels, I demonstrate the belay, including the tie-off. Students then rappel and belay each other in turn, under my supervision. Combining all these techniques from the start seems to reinforce the learning process through instruction and repetition. Students see the knots in action and tie them several times. It may seem like a lot of complicated procedures to learn at once, but when presented as a whole unit of instruction, it is easily grasped, and quite safe.

Tying off the leader. As the belayer, you are a component of the belay chain, but you have to be able to extricate yourself in an emergency. The idea is to secure the rope above you. Start by locking off the belay to free your hands. In this sequence, Craig has caught the fall by locking off the Sticht plate and then used an overhand loop knot to tie off the plate and free his hands.

Second, he attaches a Prusik to the rope and clips it to his anchor. Now he can escape from the system and connect the rope directly to the anchor. Were he cheeky enough to use a body belay, he would lock off the rope by wrapping it around his leg on the brake-hand side, then use the Prusik in the same manner.

It is important to know a variety of techniques in belaying and rappelling, including the most basic hip belays and the classic body rappel (the Dulfersitz). You should not be dependent on one piece of equipment. Experimenting with carabiner brake or carabiner wrap rappels does not take that much more time.

Body rappel. There were no volunteers for these shots — the idea of rope running over certain vital portions of the anatomy captures the imagination — so here I am. Knowledge of the body rappel, or Dulfersitz, is essential: what if the leader falls headfirst and loses his gear rack? The body rappel is tricky: if you screw up you are gone, *so practice this with a belay before you have to do it in earnest. The rope passes between your legs, over the thigh, then over the opposite shoulder, and is held by the brake hand against the hip. Two cautions: the leg wrapped in the rope must be kept lower than the other leg, or you may simply fall out of the rope, and you have to keep the rope down on your shoulder, as you will be hurting if it creeps up onto your neck.*

Carabiner brake assembly being used for rappel. This is good to know for emergencies, but not handy for day-to-day use: it takes time to set it up for each rappel, you can screw it up, and it kinks the rope. The friction wears grooves in your carabiners, and since the gates are side-loaded, they soon cease to open and close smoothly. The rope is pulled up through a pair of carabiners with the gates opposed. The carabiner to be used as the brake bar is clipped across the stacked 'biners and under the rope. Ovals work much better than Ds.

SKILLS   53

Additional knots are handy. The simple overhand is a good tie-off for the tail (the working end) of a bowline or figure-eight. The classic bowline with its many variations makes a quick, adjustable anchor. Two knots for an adjustable belay loop are the clove hitch and the belayer's knot. The belayer's knot is preferable, since there is no risk that the rope will jump onto the carabiner gate, like a poorly tied clove hitch, and a single loop goes through the attaching carabiner, rather than the two loops of the clove hitch. The belayer's knot is a bit harder to adjust than the clove hitch. Lastly, the ring bend or water knot (for webbing) can be useful, as well as the simple girth hitch and overhand loop.

The more complicated knots like the butterfly are probably unnecessary, thanks to the strength of modern ropes. Knots just can't weaken them enough to be a cause of great concern. But the strengths of the knots themselves vary. This table gives the strengths of some common knots when they are tied in climbing rope.

Knot strength in kernmantle climbing rope

no knot	100%
figure eight	75%–80% (8%–10% loss if incorrectly tied)
bowline	70%–75% (5% increase if double eye loop)
double fisherman's (grapevine)	65%–70%
water knot	60%–70%
clove hitch	60%–65%

Source: Setnicka, Timothy J. *Wilderness Search and Rescue.* Boston: Appalachian Mountain Club, 1980.

3

THE BELAY SYSTEM

First, a word about falls, which is what the belay system is all about. Falls caught by the belay system have varying impact forces, depending upon the distance fallen, the amount of rope paid out, and the mass of the climber. For a 180-pound mass the ultimate fall will generate an impact force of 2,300 pounds. A quick look at the drawing on page 66 will give you an idea of how all this works. The goal is to absorb the impact force without failure of the belay.

The components of the belay system:

- A safe, secure stance for the belayer.
- The belayer himself.
- A nondirectional anchor capable of withstanding 2,300 pounds of impact force (known as I).
- Rope, under the belayer's control.
- Running belay anchors capable of withstanding up to twice the impact force ($2I$), or 4,600 pounds.

Stance

To ensure a successful belay, the first requirement is a safe, secure stance for the belayer. *Safe* means reasonably free from rock-fall and out of the path of equipment dropped by the leader — a criterion that's often difficult to satisfy, given that the belayer must also be able to see and hear the leader. You have to weigh these two concerns and make a judgment call.

Another concern is the path of the rope as it leaves the belayer. It would be a mistake for the belayer to be where the rope would be pulled across a sharp edge in case of a fall. This might be obvious if that edge were a flake or a corner, but it is much less obvious when it is the ledge at your feet while you're belaying a second from above, or when it is the edge of an overhang or roof, which could saw the rope after the leader pulls it and places protection above.

Secure means a position that will not cause failure of the belay under impact force. The belayer and the leader share the responsibility for ensuring the integrity of the belay. As the belayer, you should have your brake hand toward the anchor, since you will tend to be pulled to that side if the anchor is not directly behind you. You should be at the end of your tie-in, so that the force of a fall doesn't jerk you out there and shock-load the anchor. The stance should allow you to be comfortable and put you in a position to best use your body to withstand impact.

A stance that would allow you to smash your head on an overhang is every bit as insecure as a shaky anchor. Keep the anchor taut: if you're tied in with enough slack to be pulled off a ledge, you're not likely to do your job. The tie-in should be selected with an eye toward its position after impact: anticipate the direction of pull in a fall. Belays, like their anchors, should be nondirectional. If you are standing on the ground belaying a leader and protection has been placed, the force would be upward, toward the protection. If that protection is not straight above you, there will be some pull sideways. If there are multiple protection points, some of which rip out in the fall, there could be several pulls in different directions.

So even in this simplest case of a belayer on the ground, it is hard to predict the direction of the pull. The only thing that can be said for sure is that it would not just be upward. In subsequent belays, the most efficient belay would hold downward pulls from the second as he climbs up, and upward pulls from the leader on the next pitch, as well as forces sideways or even straight out.

Belayer

In primitive roped climbing, the belayer was the anchor. Although we have progressed a great deal, the best method is still to have the belayer as part of the anchor. We have equipment that allows us to construct anchors to hold falls statically, without yielding an inch, but the resulting impact would often be too much for the human body on the other end of the rope, or for the rock around the anchors. Even modern technology can't do much about rock or location of internal organs, so falls have to be held dynamically.

One of the best ways to absorb impact force is to make it move a stationary object, like the belayer's body. Motion, of course, does not mean the belayer must be sent flying through the air. A well-braced belayer may feel only a slight tug — no searing of flesh down to the bone, no crippling burns, no blood oozing down the rope — just the sensation of the pull on the rope and a little pressure from the brake hand.

If the belayer is securely braced at the end of his anchor, his body is at rest. Just getting the stretch out of the anchor material and the slightest motion of the body is enough to absorb a great amount of impact force. Putting an object in motion only a fraction of an inch requires a great deal of energy.

For this reason, the belayer should always be part of the belay system. The body belay can be used, or a belay device combined with a harness or swami. Add security to the body belay by running the belay rope through a carabiner on the weak-hand side of the waist loop. One caution about a body belay: never allow any moving rope, such as the rope going to a climber, to run directly across another nylon surface, such as your anchor sling. Failure could be quick and tragic, as even a few inches of running rope could melt the runner.

Bob is belaying the leader. The Sticht plate is attached to his harness. From his tie-in he connected a loop of the climbing rope to the anchor. He is facing the direction of the probable pull of a fall and does not have any slack in his attachment to the anchor. The two trees and perlon runner are very solid, but I would add a second carabiner, gate reversed and opposed to the one in use. Bob's brake hand is palm up — much easier to manipulate the rope, but not as effective in catching a fall as palm down. Note that when he catches the fall and the plate locks up, he changes his hand. With practice it is easy to rotate the hand while locking the plate down.

THE BELAY SYSTEM

Some people are better belayers than others. It helps to pay a certain amount of attention to the leader. This is sometimes harder than one might think. Even the best of leaders spend some amount of time doing things that are not terribly interesting, like resting, selecting a nut, and whimpering. When the leader is out of sight entirely, this can be a problem. Fortunately, most rope manufacturers have given us a solution. They put some kind of pattern in the rope, like the so-called Hollywood rattlesnake. Focusing on this pattern, you can detect any motion at quite a distance because the pattern will blur. You need be only semiconscious for the phenomenon to have effect. With this kind of warning you can pay out enough rope so that the leader doesn't feel like he is in a tug-of-war. You can also watch the carabiner on the last visible piece. It will move and give away rope movement.

It's a good idea to have the middle of your rope marked, so that you can tell the leader when he has reached halfway. You should also keep him informed how much rope he has left. With experience you will learn to distinguish a 20-foot pile of rope from a 10-foot pile. The leader may be deciding if he can make a ledge in this pitch, and such information would be vital.

Anchor

When most people think of a belay, they are thinking of the anchor for the belay. As we have already seen, it should be nondirectional and capable of withstanding the impact force of a fall. The belayer is connected to it, and the point of attachment must be secure. Single carabiners may be used to connect individual points of protection to an anchor sling, but links from the anchor to the belayer should be more secure: a knot, or screwgate carabiner, or two carabiners with gates reversed and opposed. The consequences of a carabiner gate forced open would be catastrophic, if only for the loss of strength in a carabiner with an open gate.

Every link in the chain must be secure. Take care to avoid loading a carabiner on the minor axis. Strength in this direction is only a fraction of the rated strength on the main axis. To get a nondirectional belay, use either nondirectional anchors or directional points (nuts) combined in opposition. Usually, any belay anchor should have three good points. But climbing is judgment; if you think a single point is absolutely bombproof (like a sling around a tree or a block) then exercise your judgment and go with it, rather than scratch around for additional points.

To get a nondirectional anchor to withstand the forces of a fall, it is often best to arrange some equalizing system. The simplest is to make all the attaching slings the right length to meet at a central point under equal tension. You can combine runners, tying some off with knots to get the right lengths.

For two points, or two systems of points, you can simply connect them with a runner with a single twist in the center. You then clip them through the X formed by the twist; this is the point of attachment to an equalized system.

Lastly, you can take a long runner and construct an equalizing system. Doubled carabiners are clipped to the point of attachment; the safety carabiner is clipped into the loop, rather than over it, in case all but one point should fail.

A final concern is the angle of the sling at the attachment point. If it is less than 90 degrees, the force on each point will be less than the total force of the fall. An additional point that doesn't change the angle will reduce the force on each point still further. If the angle were increased, the force transmitted to each point would be increased. At 120 degrees, the force at each point is equal to the force of the fall. Any angle over 120 degrees transmits a force greater than the actual fall. So it is possible to actually weaken an anchor by adding a marginal extra point that increases the angle of the anchor sling.

To decrease the angle, you can simply make the runner longer and move the belay away from the anchor points. A rule of thumb to avoid increasing force is to make the attachment point as far away from the rock surface as the points are far apart. Another way to look at it: the angle at the attachment point should be 90 degrees or less.

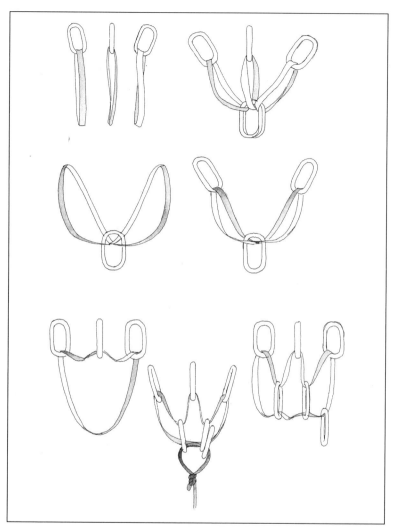

Three ways to get safe, nondirectional anchors. TOP, slings of equal length share equally in absorbing the force of impact. CENTER, this arrangement requires the least equipment, is the fastest to set up, and works with just two anchor points. BOTTOM, you need a long runner and lots of carabiners. The extra 'biner at bottom right is an added precaution, in case two of the anchor points fail.

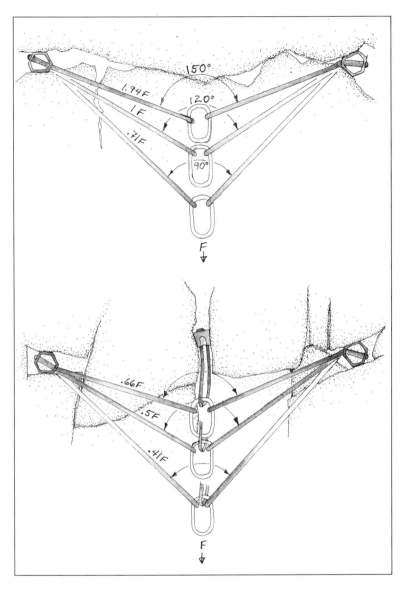

Anchor point angles and force calculations. The longer the runner, the less force there is on the anchor points. Adding a third anchor point doesn't change the angles, but it does decrease the force on each point.

But it is often not possible to move outward very far: if you're on a ledge, you can go only so far. The solution is to employ equalization techniques to the maximum. Evaluate each anchor point to see how much it is adding to your system and how it changes the configuration of the anchor as a whole. Remember, your extended thumb and forefinger form about a 90-degree angle. If your anchor sling has a greater angle, consider taking some kind of action to decrease it.

Rope

The fourth element of the belay system is the rope. Modern perlon ropes absorb much of the force of the fall. No such rope has ever broken, although some have been cut. Rope is only as good as the belayer who is handling it, though, and he must be in control. It should be coiled within reach, so that any snags can be dealt with, and it should be secure from rockfall. A neat coil, made while taking in rope, can simply be turned over if the second is not going to lead through. If you are swinging leads, the belayer simply pays out the rope, reversing the coil he made. Efficiency at this comes with practice. Having to unsnarl the rope at every belay stance is the worst possible waste of time.

Avoid hanging the slack over the edge of a ledge. If there is very little room, you will have to hang the rope, but carefully look over where it's going to be hanging before you start to take it in. You may have to hang it in sections so that it does not extend its full length into a tree or other potential snag. Sometimes you can rig a convenient anchor for the rope. Make a quick clove hitch in a loop of slack and clip the rope in, so that the loops hanging out in space are much shorter. This is easy to do in a hanging belay and can save you a lot of trouble.

The consequences of having a rope snag a distance below you can be severe. I was once in the cave at the south end of Seneca Rocks waiting for the weather to clear enough to climb. Two people had decided to risk it and had gone up on a very airy, traversing climb above me on the exposed south end of the rock. At the end of the second pitch was a small belay stance where a hanging belay is most comfortable. This stance was about 50 feet or so above the cave. I had done the same climb myself, following a British friend across to that stance, where I found his two 9mm ropes in short coils clipped into anchors. He had learned the trick climbing on Cornish sea cliffs, where high winds and seas can do nasty things to ropes. These two climbers, however, hadn't had the benefit of training on a Cornish sea cliff. Sitting inside the cave to escape the drizzle, I noticed a loop of rope appear, then lengthen as the second followed over to the stance. The loop hung in midair as the leader started up the last pitch. As the belayer took the rope upward and the winds picked up, the rope snagged hopelessly in the top branches of a tree. The leader was stuck in the rain, unable to go up or down, in the midst of a vertical pitch of 5.7 rock. The belayer had to tie him off before he could struggle with the rope. No amount of tugging would free it, so he had to rappel down to the snag in the tree, free the rope, then prusik back up to the belay, carefully taking up loops of slack, clipping them to his harness as he went. It was an all-day epic. They were just lucky there was no electrical activity in the storm, so they ended up only dripping wet, not fried.

Running belay anchors

The last components of the belay are the running belay anchors, or runners. They must be able to withstand twice the impact force, which can be as much as 4,600 pounds. Most climbers don't think of using equalizing techniques or opposition in runners, but such tactics may be even more important here. First, forces may be greater. Second, pull will invariably come from several directions in the course of a climb. Rope drag can pull upward or sideways. The highest placement will probably be pulled straight down in a fall, but lower pieces will have more outward pull, while the first placement will be pulled straight out with some force, and can even be pulled up and out. If it goes, the others may zipper out from the sudden shift in the rope. It is therefore important (read: vital) to get a good, solid, nondirectional placement as soon as possible in a pitch. This provides a directional anchor for the belay and adds security for higher pieces. The need for this directional placement

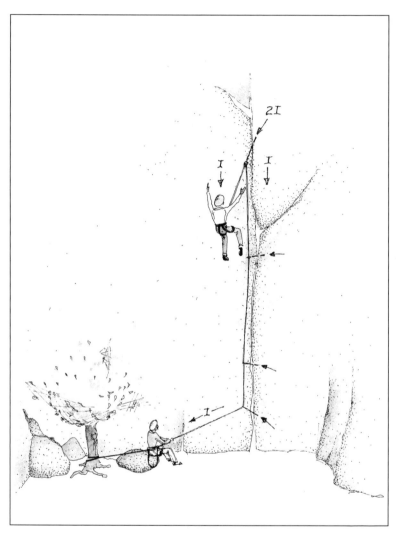

Impact force (I) *calculations. The more impact force absorbed by the belayer, the less force there is at each anchor. Still, there is considerable force — 2I — at the top runner. Here's the equation: distance fallen ÷ rope paid out = fall factor (0 to 2). In a force-2 fall, our 180-pound climber would generate 2,288 pounds of I. The tree, then, must hold 2,300 pounds; the top runner, 4,600 pounds.*

ROCK SPORT

must be weighed against the rope drag it might cause later. You always want to avoid friction of the rope over any rock surface when placing protection.

As far as equalizing protection placements, remember how easy it is to put one twist in a runner. "Quickdraw" 5-foot runners come already arranged for this. Simply unclip one strand from the bottom and connect each loop to a nut or pin.

Using the belay anchor as the first point of protection is a technique that should be used very sparingly. The impact force on the anchor might be greatly increased, but the belay might be better aimed. You clip a runner and the leader's end of the rope directly to the belay anchor. This practice is often considered when a pitch starts with an overhang or turns a corner. If the anchor is bomb-proof, the angles are awkward, and the climbing is tricky, you might consider clipping a runner into the belay. This technique is much used in ice climbing.

To conduct the best belay, give thought to each component of the system. Security is not cumulative. You are only as safe as the weakest link in the chain. All the anchors are of no avail if you pick a stance subject to rockfall or leave too much slack in the tie-in. And being careful about protection will not make up for sloppy rope handling.

4

ANCHOR POINTS

Some anchor points are easily implemented, like slinging a chickenhead. Others are more laborious, such as drilling a bolt hole for twenty minutes. All anchors are not created equal, and skill at spotting marginal ones can add up to safety and confidence when you're on difficult ground.

Natural protection

Natural features can become anchors by using the simplest climbing tool, the runner. Don't overlook the obvious, like that great big tree, for example. It makes a nondirectional anchor, often sufficient for a belay in itself. Not many climbers would fail to use a conveniently placed tree as a belay anchor, but often you may be at a loss as to how to make some trees work for you without any equipment or extra rope drag. Simply keeping the rope to the inside of the tree — opposite the direction of any fall — makes the tree a running belay point. The rope will come tight around the tree in the event of a fall. This could be a little hard on the rope, but on easy ground, such as a traverse across a ledge, this technique is very fast and provides adequate protection against the unlikely fall. This also provides protection for the second.

Use the same idea on a rock ridge with gendarmes, or seracs in an icefall. Rope drag and use of equipment are minimized.

It seems painfully obvious, but if you do use a sling around a tree, place it low on the trunk to maximize the strength of the anchor. The exceptions to this rule are dictated by the direction of the route. If a low placement would create excessive rope drag, then move the sling up on the trunk; it will probably slide down low on the trunk anyway if a fall occurs. Use tree limbs if the route wanders off from the anchor.

Don't hesitate to use small vegetation if the root systems run far down into the cracks; these can be a lot stronger than they look. I often use even dead vegetation as an anchor point to prevent upward pull on small wired nuts. A ½-inch runner hitched to a twig of mountain laurel can provide a lot of security for the small wired nut slotted in the crack directly below it. Once, while looking around for a rappel point, my Scottish climbing partner selected a bush. "It's a bloody great big thing," he said. "Got leaves and everything."

So much for the flora. All attempts to enlist the aid of local fauna in the protection system seem to have failed miserably, so we can omit any discussion of this. Let it suffice to say that pigeons are uncooperative at best, and the only copperheads one wants to see are on the hardware rack.

You may recall, however, that you are climbing on this tough stuff called rock. Many of its features—horns, spikes, chickenheads, blocks, cracks, flakes, knobs—can be used as protection. The classic is the large block; simply loop a sling over it. This is the quickest and among the strongest uses of a runner. It is necessary to check the block for sharp edges that could cut the sling and be certain the runner will stay on. Flat webbing has less tendency to slide off blocks, so it is useful to have one double runner (10 feet or so) of flat 1-inch webbing. This is almost as strong as 1-inch tubular, but it is lighter, cheaper, and longer wearing. Don't use too stiff a flat webbing, as this is intended for étriers (aiders) and sewn harnesses.

A horizontal crack forming a blocklike flake can be used in several ways. A chock can be slotted into the crack, with a runner underneath it. The runner is clipped into the rope first, and the chock may be clipped into the runner or into the rope, as circumstances dictate. The chock is holding the runner down in the crack.

One can also use a real rock as a chockstone to perform the same function. Don't hesitate to use some natural chocks. Historically, this is how "clean" climbing began, and there is no reason not to continue the practice. The rocks littering a mountain ledge could be the material for your belay. On alpine climbs with minimal gear, these are an important source of protection. By using such rocks, you may be able to save your few chocks for runners instead of leaving them as part of the belay. You may just be sitting on a rock that'll work like a #42 hex. Select a firm rock without sharp edges and work it around in the crack until it fits.

In slinging a natural chockstone or block you have several options. The simplest and strongest is to loop the runner over the object. This employs the full loop strength of the runner.

The next strongest method is to thread the runner around the object and clip it doubled, either to the rope or to another runner. This avoids the loss of strength that a knot would entail, and it is twice as strong as a girth hitch.

Your third option is to use a knot in the sling. The girth hitch is quick and often works well, but it depends on a loop formed with two layers of webbing. These two layers may be more prone to slippage than would a single layer. To obtain a single-layer loop, use an overhand loop knot. This knot allows the sling to be cinched up around the object and is less likely to loosen than a girth hitch. The overhand loop can be used on an old, much-abused pin, or piton, whose eye has broken off. The shaft may still be quite strong, but don't blame me if some rotten old pin doesn't hold your fall.

A runner can also be used to sling a narrow spot in a crack. The knot may be jammed behind a constriction. This is also useful for keeping runners in place around flakes.

Slinging a block. The doubled runner is stronger than a girth hitch. Rope drag is a concern here — it might cause the runner to slip out. I might move the sling's knot so that it jams against the rock on the right.

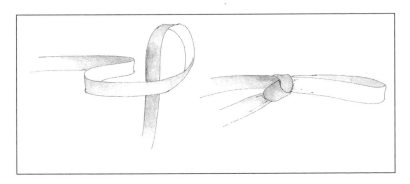

The overhand loop, used to cinch a webbing runner around a piton or natural protection. The loop is tightened around the object, and then the knot itself is tightened, making it very secure. Unlike the girth hitch, a single loop goes over the object, making the runner less likely to slip off.

Two blocks. Since they make firm contact, you can thread the sling around the point of contact, and it can't come off. Check such blocks for sharp edges that could cut the sling.

A runner is no good unless it stays on, at least until you can place other protection. The primary way to achieve this is to correctly match the material to the situation. For small flakes, 2-foot loops of ½-inch runner or 3 feet of 9/16-inch supertape can come in handy. Larger objects will take 1-inch tubular webbing. Flat webbing may work better on smooth knobs. Sewn runners are often more stable because there is no bulging knot to prevent full contact around the knob. My personal choice is Troll Supertape, a flat, solid, superstrong sewn runner. Troll's ⅝-inch tape is as strong as a tied 1-inch tubular runner, but much lighter.

The chief cause of losing a runner is rope drag. If you take the usual steps to minimize rope drag, the runner will stay secure. You simply use a long enough runner to allow the sling to sit quietly. Using the heaviest of your carabiners (or perhaps two of them) to weight the sling down at its point of attachment to the rope may suffice. Consider using a nut and its sling to connect runner and rope. Clip in above and below the nut with the nut nearest the rope. Extra gear (which you hope you won't need) will weigh down the runner.

Don't overlook the possibility that you can slot a small wired nut in an upward direction below the runner. In this way a tiny wired nut may afford bombproof protection. I always carry the #0 and #1 RPs for just such uses. They don't take up much room when racked with the rest of the RPs, and their weight is negligible. Small nuts may also be used as directional anchors to change the path of the rope, minimizing sidepulls that could work against the protection. Though such nuts would be ripped out by a hard fall, they may work long enough to allow a good runner to do its job. Another runner could be used to hold the primary protection in place just as the chock is used, slotted upward or sideways. The key is to be aware of all the options, and keep in mind how the system will work with rope drag during the climb and under impact in the event of a fall.

When girth-hitching an object, remember to turn the hitch in such a way that rope drag or impact will not cause the knot to pull the runner off. The overhand loop is not prone to such behavior. It is little known because it was used primarily in aid climbing. Since younger free climbers have little or no experience with aid techniques, they may remain ignorant of this.

More discussion of sizes and materials for runners is in Chapter 7, on equipment.

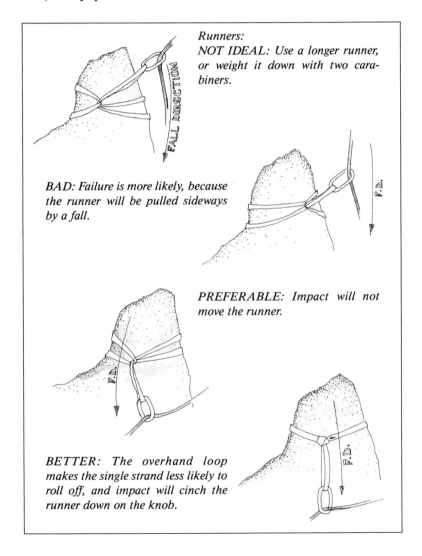

Runners:
NOT IDEAL: Use a longer runner, or weight it down with two carabiners.

BAD: Failure is more likely, because the runner will be pulled sideways by a fall.

PREFERABLE: Impact will not move the runner.

BETTER: The overhand loop makes the single strand less likely to roll off, and impact will cinch the runner down on the knob.

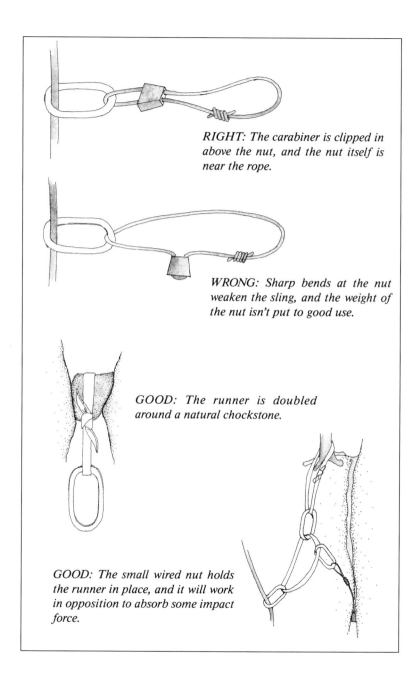

RIGHT: The carabiner is clipped in above the nut, and the nut itself is near the rope.

WRONG: Sharp bends at the nut weaken the sling, and the weight of the nut isn't put to good use.

GOOD: The runner is doubled around a natural chockstone.

GOOD: The small wired nut holds the runner in place, and it will work in opposition to absorb some impact force.

Quick and easy

All this discussion of natural protection may have little relevance to you if you are already on a steady diet of 5.9 finger cracks. If that is all you ever intend to do, that is fine, but most crag climbers expand their horizons at some time. The techniques of natural protection were refined for British crag climbing, but they assume their greatest importance today in alpine climbing.

In alpine climbing, the tools at your disposal are limited, as is the time you can safely allow for any climb. Natural protection is simple and quick, two virtues in any climbing situation.

Saving your skin doesn't have to mean setting up complicated systems of protection. Two friends of mine were climbing a rock ridge. They were excellent climbers with first ascents on Eastern crags to their credit. They were moving simultaneously, roped together by two 9mm ropes, as on an easy snow or ice climb. They were accustomed to third-classing routes, and their technique would have been suitable for a soft snow slope. On snow, a fall by one climber can be arrested by the other. This, however, was rock. Although it was easy 5.3 rock, and a route they had done many times, the leader pulled off a loose block. One rope was cut. The other rope pulled his second off. One man fell about 60 feet before the rope snagged on something to arrest his progress, the other went the full 200 feet.

Result: one serious injury, one death.

Had they wanted to solo, they should not have roped up. Still, they could have climbed simultaneously and been roped together if the leader had been placing some protection, so the rope could have done them some good. In this situation slinging horns and blocks and clipping fixed pitons would have been infinitely safer and not much less convenient. A leader with a fair number of slings can go a long way on easy rock before having to stop and retrieve his slings from the second. They could have climbed hundreds of feet almost as fast, and in much greater safety.

It is always germane to ask yourself, "What the hell am I doing? And why?"

One final note on runners. Remember that the climbing rope can form the runner for the belay anchor. If you have the slack, you can run the rope around an object, then tie in to the back of the harness with a figure-eight knot, figure-eight loop, or a belayer's hitch tied into a carabiner clipped to the harness.

Chocks

Chocks are directional devices. Chockcraft is the art of making chocks into secure, nondirectional anchors. On the face of it, chockcraft appears deceptively simple. Place the chock in a crack above a constriction, pull down until it jams, then clip into the rope. The more chocks in a placement, the more secure one is; the bigger the chock, the stronger it is.

Sometimes it really is that simple, and that is the attraction of chocks. This is why they have largely replaced pitons on the American climbing scene. Before the 1970s, chocks were almost completely unheard of. Few were produced, and most of those were imported from Britain. Today it is hard to find a climber who has ever driven a piton, and anyone contemplating the use of one is regarded as something of a leper.

Unfortunately, the demise of the piton has not led to a generation of climbers who protect wisely and climb according to the character of the rock. The airhead who climbs with a fortune in Friends and wired wedges, setting each one with a hernia-inducing pull, is no better than the mighty Thor who nailed his way up routes a few years ago.

It's not that these people are morally inferior to some imaginary pure, clean climber. The problem is that sooner or later the tool won't work, or it will take so long to work that the climb won't be accomplished. Carefully practiced, however, chockcraft will make you a more versatile climber, able to do more kinds of climbs, and a little safer besides.

So much for the sermon. Now on to the practice of chockcraft. There are two types of chocks, *wedges* and *cams*; both can be either active or passive.

Chocks are not just for cracks. They can be slipped behind flakes, or between surface irregularities in the rock. In some limestones, solution pockets occur, and in conglomerates a pebble may wear out of the surrounding rock, leaving a neat hole. These cavities will often take a cam chock. It takes a bit of fiddling to place the chock in a position so that it won't just drop out, but these placements are often among the strongest against a downward pull.

Chocks are best employed in vertical cracks, but they can work quite well in horizontal cracks as well. Find a spot where the outside of the crack is fairly wide, and slide the chock in sideways, to an area of the crack with a narrower outside edge. With luck, internal con-

Hex cammed into a horizontal crack. Downward force just sets it harder, so it is well placed.

striction in the crack can be used to prevent the chock from sliding back. A classic case is using a stopper in its narrow aspect, then turning it to its wider wedge side, secure against both outward and sideways pulls. The main force of the fall will pull straight out on the chock, but the protection system often exerts forces in other directions. These may not be obvious at first glance, so it is best to examine any chock placement with an eye toward nondirectional security.

In vertical cracks the chock is wedged for a downward pull, but it should also be secure against upward pull from rope drag, and against a pull straight out from a fall held by higher protection. If it can't withstand these forces, the placement is not secure. Always think ahead to the possible location of the next placement.

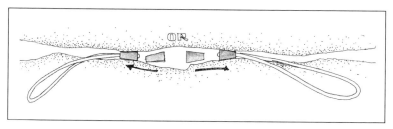

Horizontal cracks. If you're moving left, insert the nut at the wide spot and slide it left; or if you're moving right, slide it to the right. A crack with a lip on the outside edge makes the placement more secure.

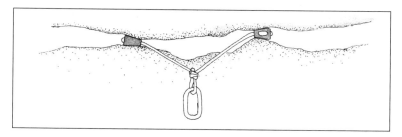

Another horizontal crack. Opposition can make two marginal placements work and also give a nondirectional anchor point. To keep the two nuts secure, maintain the tension between them by twisting the slings or shortening them with standard knots.

The loyal opposition

Chocks, remember, are inherently directional anchors, but the best protection is obtained from nondirectional anchors. This is true whether the anchor is part of the belay stance, or just a runner. The classic method of obtaining a nondirectional chock anchor is through opposition. The two opposed chocks hold each other in place, and this tension works against outside force.

Sometimes the opposed chocks need not be in constant tension. The opposition has to work only in case of substantial force. In more extreme cases the tension must be maintained by precise connection of the chocks. This can be accomplished through the selection of slings and carabiners so that the two can just barely be connected. To adjust sling length and maintain tension, a girth hitch or overhand loop knot may be used. Shorten the chock slings with overhand knots. This technique may also be used to concentrate the force of the fall on the part of the chock that's deepest in the crack (important in very shallow cracks). It was fashionable at one time to carry a small cross-section of automobile inner tube to create this situation, and the idea may still have merit in certain situations.

Opposed chocks can be connected in several ways to vary the amount of force taken by each chock. At one extreme, one chock could take most of the force and merely be held in place against rope drag by its counterpart. At the other extreme, the force on the chocks is carefully equalized and tensioned just to hold them both in the crack.

Play around with opposing nuts at ground level until you can do the full range, from one extreme to the other. It could be important. Once, I went to do one of the moderate climbs at Seneca Rocks. My partner wanted to lead, so we took his rack. When we reached the start of the crux pitch, we found that the cracks were much larger than any of our nuts. They were rotten inside, too, so we didn't like the idea of using the internal flakes for our belay. We moved along a narrow, airy ledge to a vertical corner, where the climb started in earnest. The vertical crack had one dubious-looking pin, and our nuts just wobbled around. We played with opposition, but the nuts

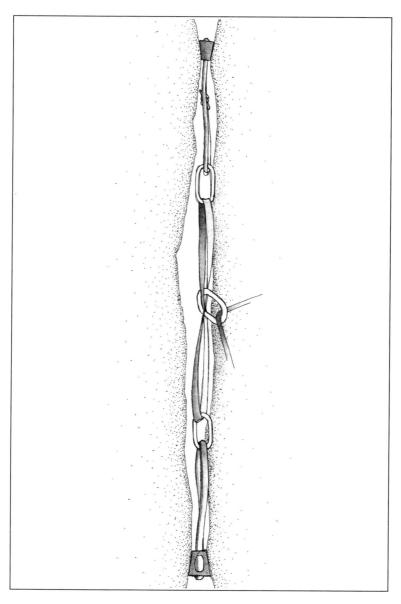

Opposition. To equalize force between the anchors, clip into the runner where the strands cross. Voilà: a nondirectional anchor.

would not hold each other in a position to hold an outward pull. We began to doubt; it seemed that both of us, despite all our years of climbing experience, were being psyched out by this crack. We both stared in frustration at the crack until I experimented with twisting one sling, then sliding it through the other sling to provide the tension that would hold the nuts together. We both let out an involuntary "Ahhh." Everything was all right, and we could continue. Clipping the tensioned anchor to the pin made the whole mess bombproof, and we proceeded to have a first-rate time on this classic climb. It had taken the two of us about 45 minutes of scratching around to get it right, but there was no question that it was worth it, not only for the satisfaction of the moment, but also for the feeling of confidence it gave us.

That was a long time to get a belay—too long. The point is to practice such techniques in your climbing every day, so that when you really need them, they come naturally and quickly. You don't want to be on that ledge trying to remember a picture in this book.

Speaking of pictures, there are some general principles illustrated by the photos that should be examined in more detail. Simple wedge chocks are the most secure and often the strongest. Closely examine each placement to determine the amount of contact between nut and rock. The more contact, the stronger the placement. There is less likelihood that the rock or the soft alloy of the nut will be sheared away.

The angle of contact must also be determined. If the plane of the nut and the side of the crack are parallel, there is less chance that the nut will shear out or rotate under force and pop out. Rotation is a problem in many types of cracks, so manufacturers modify their wedges. Campbell used a central groove in their Saddle Wedges, and Chouinard curves the sides of the larger stoppers. British chocks, called Rocs, first employed this form. In smaller sizes such shapes stick too well and are very difficult to remove. Campbell warned against placing their wedges endwise; Chouinard keeps the ends fairly narrow, where they are less likely to rotate. Thus the Chouinards are a bit more versatile, giving two sizes for each stopper. The curved stoppers are not as good for this, since the area of

Bombproof placement for a stopper. The large area of contact on both faces makes rotation under impact unlikely. The crack narrows below the stopper, the rock looks firm, and the nut is set deep enough inside the crack.

contact has been greatly reduced. The newest stoppers are less curved. Bluewater makes "classic" flat-sided wedges, and there are several types of small soldered cable wedges. The Campbell-style groove has reappeared in HB nuts and DMM Wallnuts.

Somehow there is nothing more reassuring than a solid wired stopper placement. The very simplicity inspires confidence. You can see that it will work, and the cable appears bombproof. The problem with wedges is that you have to find a crack of precisely the right size. You find yourself carrying a lot of wedges to increase your chances of having the right wedge at the right time. And wedges are heavy. Newer-style stoppers are more carefully constructed to be lighter in each size and even have improved cables.

Wedging out

Removing a wedge usually means simply pushing it back up and out of the crack. Pushing up on the base of the wedge with the fingers should do the job. If the nut has been set, a nut tool is useful to take the abuse your fingers shouldn't. Start with your hands and go to a tool as the next resort. Wired chocks can be pushed up by the wire if the nut is epoxied to the top of the cable. Of course, single-wire nuts don't need this refinement.

If the cable is not epoxied to the nut, it can be pulled up from above, and the chock removed with upward jerks. This will also work for perlon or webbing-slung chocks if the fit of the runner to the nut is not too tight. Taping the wires or perlon together just below the nut can substitute for the epoxy, and leaves the sling free for other uses. However, a number of passes around the sling are needed and the tape doesn't last long.

If the crack has edge constrictions, you must first loosen the nut, then find where it was put into the crack and retrieve it. With small wired nuts this can be a delicate process. The end of a nut tool can cradle a small nut back in a crack where your fingers can't reach. The Leeper is thinner than other tools, yet it is very strong and will stand up to years of abuse. There seems to be no good way to carry it, but nothing works like it for retrieving nuts.

If the nut is set so badly that it won't budge despite all of these measures, then simply grab the wire or sling and jerk it upward. This may unseat the nut (and you as well) and make it possible to manipulate. The risk here lies in the fact that you are pivoting the top of the wedge. This widest part may stick higher and deeper in the crack, worsening the situation.

Brass nuts are more prone to sticking in placements and should not be forcefully set. Campbell chocks were softer than Chouinard, and a bit more sticky. Forrest copper nuts also stick, but this is part of their appeal. Soldered wire nuts should not be jerked upward for removal, since this can damage the soldered joints. It is important to be more careful removing these nuts; their cables are more likely to fray and can be damaged by a nut tool. The softer brass of some of these nuts can complicate the process.

If all else fails, get a rock and hammer the nut tool to loosen the chock. If you climb with someone who cannot refrain from setting his nuts, carry a hammer (like Chouinard's Crag Hammer or the Forrest Mjollnir) in addition to the nut pick. When you give him back his smashed nuts, he may begin to get the idea.

Wired

Some climbers will not consider anything but wired stoppers; others won't have them on the rack. The wires are strong, durable, and allow some manipulation of the nut with more precision than perlon or webbing. Good stiff perlon can act as a wire. Wired nuts are much more prone to levering out from rope drag. Of course, this can be solved with a runner, but some climbers don't like carrying the extra equipment. Kevlar cord and Spectra are other options. These are lighter than wire and offer more flexibility. They are nowhere near as flexible as regular perlon, but they are stronger.

I always figure a good wedge will need a runner anyway, so what's the difference? In smaller sizes, the wire is the only way to go. Girth-hitching a runner to a wire is a very poor practice, since the cable will cut right through webbing. If you can't use a carabiner, at least feed the webbing through doubled.

Hex signs

The Hexentric is a bit more difficult to place than a simple wedge, but it offers a greater variety of placements and more versatility. Hexes are the most efficient chocks, if weight is a concern. There is no denying that they take a bit of getting used to, but in the larger sizes of cracks they are just about the only option.

The hex offers four attitudes and sizes of placements for each nut, while the wedge offers two at best. There is a logical progression in the size of each deployment of each nut. With time, these become quite familiar, and a quick look at a crack will tell you what range of nuts to try.

One advantage of the hex is its cam action, which provides a degree of torque in the placement. The result is that hexes are often quite secure. The camming action of the placement protects it from being loosened by rope drag.

Super hex placement. Good contact with the rock, deep crack, and the camming action of the hex all help hold it in place.

If you are confronted with a large crack and your rack is down to smaller nuts, or if you just don't carry any mammoth chocks, you can resort to stacking nuts. Stoppers stack very easily top to bottom, on both their narrow ends and their broader sides. Hexes can be stacked either side to side, or end to end.

In all honesty I must admit that I have always sought some alternative to stacking nuts. Opposition, natural protection, or a smaller nut in some internal constriction of the crack is easier to work out. Stacking nuts is something you can try to beef up a belay

Hex placed lengthwise. The ends of the chock are tapered, giving a secure, wedgelike fit. The hex has a smaller area of contact than a wedge, but it is a lot lighter and more versatile.

stance, or an already secure placement in the climb. It is not, however, the sort of thing you can do while hanging off a hand jam. You need two hands free to work the nuts into position.

Tests conducted by John Stannard showed that stacked nuts can be quite strong.* Two stoppers stacked in a badly flaring vertical placement pulled out at 1,000 pounds. Better placements held up to 2,500 pounds.

The two nuts can be rotated slightly, so that the edge of one is contacting the plane of another. The nuts will deform if holding a fall, but they can hold surprising amounts of force. Some climbers used to put two stoppers on the same sling so that the leader could stack them. The increasing use of Friends has cut down on these tactics a lot. Active wedges work like stacked stoppers but offer limited rotation.

Pitons, or pins, can be used as removable chocks. Deep, thin cracks are ideal for finger-inserted knifeblades, and for the thinnest of the old Lost Arrow pitons. I have even seen a RURP slipped behind a flake for an aid placement, with body weight gingerly eased onto it. Pins that are not driven will work best in horizontal cracks. They work in this way like Crack'n-ups, Chouinard's tiny chocks, which enjoyed brief popularity as a free climbing tool.

When a pin is used as a chock, the blade is working like a wedge. In deep horizontal cracks, fall force will just push the end of the piton against the top of the crack. However, any rotation on the placement may pull it right out, and vibration from rope drag has to be avoided.

Pitons

Piton is now a dirty word to many free climbers. I recall a fellow doing a climb within shouting distance of me at Seneca Rocks. He wanted to know if he was on route and where he should continue. I pointed out a fixed pin that marked the route. "I never use fixed pins," he replied.

---

*The test results were published in *The Eastern Trade,* vol. 2, no. 3 (August 1973).

ROCK SPORT

That remark was delivered in a tone I thought reserved for abstinence from alcohol or other of life's little pleasures. It was as if the man feared he would be tainted by clipping into the fixed protection. Perhaps that climber wanted to preserve the feeling of climbing with only his own protection. I can understand that desire, but I would suggest that clipping fixed pins need not interfere with how you feel about a climb. I never trust a fixed piton, but I rarely pass one up. Even a rotten, battered, badly placed pin can be useful, if you know how to use it.

The piton offers one tremendous advantage to the free climber: it is usually nondirectional. It works by wedging itself in the crack like a nut. The difference is that the piton required energy to be inserted into the crack, and unless force in excess of that energy is brought to bear directly on it, it will not fail. When that happens, the pin pops out suddenly with a high-pitched ping. Sometimes pins will shift around inside a crack and realign themselves much like nuts do. Marginal placements approach the directional qualities of chocks; bomber placements are more nearly nondirectional.

Being nondirectional, pitons can give the clean climber a secure place to put a nut he can count on. That way you are trusting the fixed protection not to hold your fall, but merely to hold a nut in place. The standard angle piton was ¾ inch, the baby angle, ½ inch. If there is a fixed pin of either size, there is probably a nearby spot the same size in the crack. Insert a #7 stopper (old #5) whose wedge is ½-inch thick and, turned lengthwise, ¾ inch. With the wire or sling clipped into the eye of the piton, the stopper will not lift out from rope drag, and now you have two points for a downward pull. One old fixed pin can thus give you real confidence-inspiring protection. A directional nut placement and an untrustworthy pin are combined to give you what neither could on its own. (The #1 hex also has the ½-inch and ¾-inch sizes.)

Lost Arrow pins went up to ⅜ inch, so smaller stoppers or brass nuts can be fitted around them. The scars left by piton placement are also useful, since they are roughly a predictable size. When you see a piton scar, pull out your #7 or an old #5 stopper; it will probably fit at the bottom of the scar.

Now you know why they used pitons. This Lost Arrow sunk into a horizontal crack is a classic placement. Tiny chocks could be placed in opposition here, but the old pin is a lot more secure.

To perform this function of securing nut placement, the piton itself does not have to be a very good placement. It doesn't even have to be in very good condition, which is nice, since many old pins have been hammered so many times by climbers testing their soundness that their eyes may be deformed or gone entirely. Attempts at testing or removal may have shifted the pin to an awkward position.

Clip into a piton with a carabiner, preferably rotating the 'biner so that the gate opens out and down. This is the ideal attachment, because it limits the possibility of a failure. Anything threaded through a piton will cut if enough force is applied.

If you can't get a regular carabiner in, try an older carabiner that doesn't have the thick, blind gate of newer models, or use a thin, lightweight carabiner. If you can't get the carabiner to roll over once it's clipped in, remember that force exerted by a fall could cause the carabiner to act like a lever and pull out the pin. Careful inspection of the surrounding rock will tell you if this is likely. The gate could also be opened by a fall. Whether the open-gate strength of a carabiner is better than a runner threaded through the piton eye is a judgment call. Sometimes the pin is best with the flexible secure attachment of a threaded runner, sometimes better with the solid metal of the carabiner. If you are short of 'biners, you can always thread the pins when you have a good stance to do so. When a chock is to be combined with the pin, threading the runner may minimize the equipment committed to this placement.

You can use a wired stopper as the runner to be threaded through the eye, or the nut can be run down slightly on the cable, then cinched back up, under the shaft of an eyeless old pin. You have to weigh the loss of the stopper for this purpose against its possible use later for protection.

Use the thickest material possible to thread a pin. Double the runner and slide it through the eye. This is twice as strong as girth-hitching it. Use the girth hitch only if you really need the extra length on the runner. You can tie the pin off with a girth hitch or, better, the overhand loop. You can even clip a carabiner into the eye to prevent the loop from slipping off. The overhand loop can be used on the broken shaft of an old pin.

For tying off a piton, the overhand loop is the best knot, but the girth hitch is quicker and easier to tie with one hand. Your choice.

The accompanying illustrations show some of the options for using old pins. The value of these ideas is that they represent simple and quick contributions to the protection system. Here are the preferred attachments to fixed pins, in order of preference:

- Carabiner, gate opening out and down.
- Carabiner, any old way.
- Runner, threaded double.
- Runner, girth-hitched.
- Wired stopper, wire threaded double through the eye.
- Wired stopper, wire over the pin, nut under.
- Overhand loop or girth hitch on the shaft, with a carabiner clipped into the eye to minimize the chance the runner will slip off.

The fixed pin is the nondirectional anchor that is hard to come by with chocks, and it can be combined with the smallest, lightest tools of clean climbing — small wired nuts, hero loops, and runners — to give real protection.

In short, the piton is something for nothing. But can you trust it? I will not tell you how to drive a pin or how to remove it, but I can tell you how to evaluate those you come upon and let you decide what fixed protection can do for you.

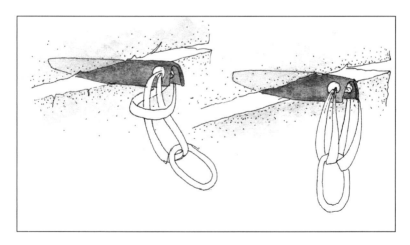

Piton options. LEFT, girth-hitched. RIGHT, the runner is doubled, then fed through. This offers twice the strength of the girth hitch.

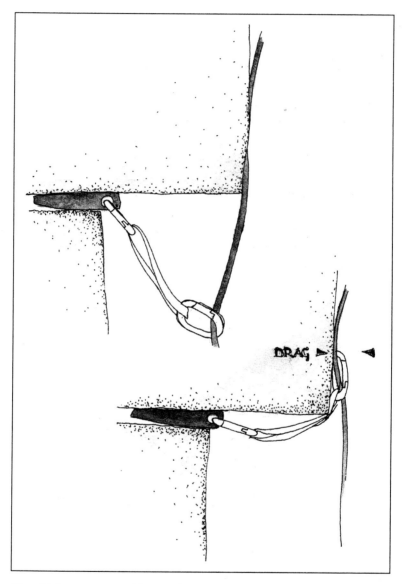

DRAG

You think you can avoid rope drag by using a runner, but when you go higher and the clip-in clears the overhang, surprise: the carabiner forces the rope against the rock. A real drag.

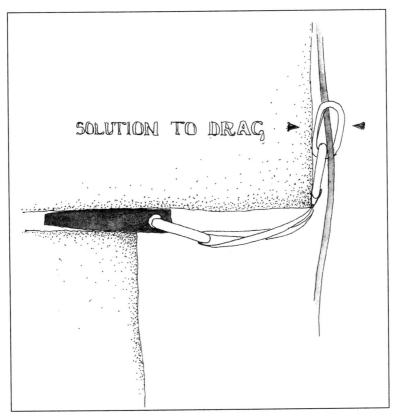

Make the runner longer and, more important, weight the end of the runner with a second carabiner. Or use a nut and its sling as part of the runner.

Checking 'em out

First, consider the placement. Pins are usually strongest when placed in opposition to fall direction—for example, in a horizontal crack for a vertical pull. Like nuts, they are best placed with constrictions on either side. The more contact with the rock, the more security. Hence a well-placed horizontal, like a Lost Arrow, driven in right up to the eye without bottoming out in the crack, is probably the most secure pin. Pins are stronger if their eyes face in the direction of any impact force.

Now, the pins themselves. Formerly, pitons were malleable, soft iron that conformed to the internal shape of the crack. They rusted quickly; this added slightly to their security while decreasing their strength.

Chrome-moly pitons were much stronger but expensive. They were made to be reused. Chrome-moly pins eventually rust slightly on the surface, and this loosens their grip. As fixed pins, they rust out and would have to be redriven. Even with surface rust, they are stronger than soft iron. In a good placement they are like a Friend, probably stronger than the rock.

Chouinard Lost Arrows and Angles are all chrome-moly; Knifeblades and Bugaboos are chrome nickel steel; Bongs are aluminum alloy. SMC chrome-moly angles have a chem-nickel plating that made them more useful as fixed pins. Their shallow angles, 0.2 inch to 0.4 inch, were useful in distorted cracks but were somewhat subject to rotation, like chocks. Angles are often under constant pressure on a small area, the blades and part of the back. Over time they can become brittle from this stress and will then fail at much below their normal load.

The best angles for fixed pins are Leeper Z pitons, since they have an additional blade to grip the rock. They can also stand up very well over a long period of time.

CMI made horizontals in various thicknesses, from Knifeblade to Lost Arrow, all with offset eyes. They are very good as fixed pins. Some European steel pins, like Charlets and Simonds, also have offset eyes. They may be chrome-moly or another steel alloy. Simond, for example, makes identical pins of both types. There is no way to tell by looking at the pin in rock which it is. Such European horizontals, if they appear not to be too old and if the plating looks good, can be very strong. Clog King Pins were nickel chrome-moly steel, gun blacked, not plated. DMM now makes the King Pins.

European angles tend to be weaker than U.S. makes. (The angle piton was invented for the U.S. Army in World War II.) Any piton with a ring can be very weak. Ring angles can either be very old Army surplus, or cheap continental pins, chiefly used for descent. Look carefully at the pin inside the rock. It may even be a ring wafer, a tiny horizontal, fixed on old aid climbs or descent routes. Any ring pin must be suspect since the welded joints of the rings were never uniformly strong. Still, I must admit I have seen several of these old ring pins hold surprisingly hard falls.

Tapping on a fixed pin will give some idea of its soundness, both through its lack of motion and the sound it makes. Bottomed-out pins and pins in rotten placements will give off a slight vibrating sound. The old saw about pounding in a pin until it gave off a ringing sound is misleading. Many great pins never made any such noise, and a pin in a flared crack will ring like Big Ben but wouldn't hold your breath.

The rock around fixed pins and bolts may rot because of weathering and stress from the hardware. Look carefully at the rock around the pin, especially near the blades of angles and right around the shafts of bolts. How long fixed hardware lasts is a function of the amount of freeze-thaw action at work, and the acidity of any soil atop the crag. This explains why hardware is long lasting at Seneca Rocks, West Virginia (where the climate is warm and soil erosion negligible, since Seneca is about three feet wide at the top), but could work out in one season on Cannon Mountain, New Hampshire (where winters are severe and soil washes down from fields of alpine tundra above the cliff).

Look for signs of previous shifts of the pin. Clip in a carabiner and runner and give a good pull outward.

If you climb long enough, you will probably have to use fixed pins or bolts, at least as rappel anchor. Since rappel failure is always serious, a little knowledge of this hardware can only help. When intelligently evaluated, old pitons can become a useful part of your protection system.

Bolts

Bolts should be used only where a blank rock face precludes other protection or the fragility of the rock makes using nuts or pins more damaging in the long run. The popular notion that bolts are permanent and secure is fundamentally false. Even stainless steel bolts corrode eventually, or at least loosen dangerously.

The two commonly used types of bolts are Rawl and Star. It is important to remember that these bolts were originally not made for climbing purposes—climbers merely adopted them for their use—and are not subject to the careful controls during manufacture that we have come to expect in climbing equipment. As for the part you clip into, the prevalent hangers are SMC and Leeper. They are well tested, strong, and not likely to act as a lever against the shaft.

Traditionally, ¼-inch and ⅜-inch Rawl bolts were most common. Rappel-placed bolts were usually ⅜ inch; ¼-inch bolts were placed on lead, with two at belays. Now 5.10 has introduced ⁵/₁₆-inch bolts and drills, which are much stronger than the ¼-inch but not so much harder to place. Like Leeper, 5.10 has to be careful about its bolts, giving you a measure of protection that your local hardware store won't.

Metolius has introduced another bolt design, with an integrated teardrop-shaped eye. PMI is distributing Petzl bolts from Europe, home of the Eurodogs and their Bosch battery-powered drills. PMI's advertisements show a carabiner being clipped into a Petzl hanger. The hand holding the 'biner has long, red fingernails; either it's a woman or that's what happens to you if you place bolts on rappel.

A good bolt is driven into firm rock until the hanger is flush with a fairly flat section of the rock surface. The hanger may spin around on some designs and placements. This is no great cause for concern. Just make sure you turn the hanger down when you clip in: you want any impact force to be parallel to the surface the hanger is mounted on. Clipping into an upside-down hanger is just creating a lever to pull the shaft out.

Inspect the bolt and its hanger for cracks, weathering around the shaft (epoxy around the top of the shaft to prevent weathering is a good sign), scars from hammer blows, or pry marks, as well as how much flat surface the hanger is making contact with.

Never hammer on a bolt. You can't drive it back in and you are just damaging the hanger. The shaft may have bottomed out if the hole wasn't drilled deep enough, and pounding will just make it recoil outward.

Bad bolts, bad news. Left and top bolts have hangers that pull straight out on the shafts. The right-hand bolt has a good hanger but is way too close to the top one. This belay is a nightmare.

Another never: never use more than two carabiners in a chain. Sometimes at two bolt belay stances, there is a temptation to do this. Three carabiners chained together can be twisted in such a way as to open the center carabiner.

An Air Voyager, or other impact-absorbing runner, can make many manky bolt belays more secure. There is one problem: multiple impacts of the bar tacks popping can open carabiner gates. Aside from the obvious risk of unclipping entirely, an open gate means a carabiner strength of under 1,000 pounds. The AV and bolt may work fine, but your carabiner breaks! The solution is a locking carabiner at each end of the AV. You might be able to get two microbiners into some shock-absorbing runners; others are sewn in a pattern that avoids popping the gate. If you are climbing a lot in a bolt-protected area (Stone Mountain, Joshua Tree, Tuolumne, Smith Rock, The Needles), give some thought to AVs and Chouinard Light D screwgates for belay stations. DMM makes a light D that opens one-handed and locks when closed. There is a T profile 'biner that can be locked open for clipping in, then locked shut. You can get only one 'biner into most bolt hangers, so why not make it a locking one?

Bolts are the last measure in protection. They should be placed only after careful consideration and exploration of alternatives. They are no stronger than other types of protection and they deteriorate over time. They should not be considered permanent anchors. Talk to the locals — they know the history of their bolts.

Anchors aren't complicated; get all you feel you need, and always think about where the next one may be. Make them as strong as conditions and time allow, and as close to nondirectional as possible. Start with fixed and natural protection, always employing the simplest and quickest solutions.

5

LEAD CLIMBING TACTICS

Climbing tactics are to a large extent determined by the nature of the climb being attempted. You would approach a 5.10 at the Gunks differently from the north face of the Grand Teton. Yet there is always one common element: time. Time is vital. No one can spend forever on a climb. It doesn't matter whether the enemy is the weather or your own waning strength. The faster and more efficient you are at the mechanics of climbing and belaying, the safer you are, and the greater your chance for success.

Saving time—being fast and efficient and safe—suggests the following basic principles for good lead climbing:

Effective rope management. You can lose time by managing the rope poorly. Untangling a rope salad at each belay is the easiest way to let a climb get the best of you. Instead, you want to simply turn over a neat pile and go on up.

Optimal use of running belays. Using natural protection and runners saves time. Arranging nondirectional belays is not only much safer, it also saves rearranging the belay for the next pitch.

Efficient, bombproof belays. Leader and belayer should have a smooth routine: gear is neatly racked, anchor is ready and waiting, belay device is operated without jams. Anything less takes time and energy — precious commodities on a climb.

The tools and techniques used to apply these principles may vary some, but the results should be the same: nobody gets hurt. The idea is to develop all the necessary skills and practice them in your everyday climbing so that they come naturally when you need them on more committing routes. Let's take each one in turn.

Rope

You have probably witnessed or, worse, been in the middle of a jammed belay device. Belay devices reduce the risk of injury but should contribute to efficiency, not detract from it. There are several causes, chief among them a rope that has not been well cared for. You have to remember that the belay is really you, that some metal gadget won't do the job for you.

There is a persistent myth that the Sticht plate, especially one with a spring, somehow works automatically. No such luck. Any device still requires the belayer to manipulate the rope carefully, inch by inch, giving it his utmost attention. Admiring the view when the leader is at a reasonably secure stance is no big deal — it is part of the experience of being in the mountains. But if your eyes glaze over and you find yourself staring at your shoes, you are no longer climbing as part of a team; you are just a glorified tourist, waiting for a top rope.

As belayer, you have to be involved in the lead. Watch for rope drag. Observe how the protection is placed so that you can remove it quickly. Think about how best to conserve strength while following. Maybe there's a section that the leader cautiously stems but that you, spared some risk by the rope from above, can do on a layback. It may be more difficult but ultimately more efficient, and safer.

Some leaders simply haul their seconds in like oversize fish. This is not a good idea. A rope under tension is susceptible to cutting, and the rope drag may cause some pieces of protection, even pieces that went in easily enough, to jam; Friends are especially prone to shifting under tension. If the second needs a tight rope, fine, but look at what he is doing — don't just lean back and reel him in.

Runners

Much of the art of leading is the selecting of running belay points, or runners. (A runner is a specific piece of equipment; the term is also used to describe protection points between belay stances.) The aim is security, but placing more runners does not always make you more secure. Runners take time and energy to place. The leader may be better served by devoting that time and energy to climbing.

It bears repeating: No climber has limitless energy or infinite time. The climb may demand more of each than you can spare. In crag climbing, reaching the limit may mean nothing more serious than having to go home when it gets dark, but in alpine climbing, it may lead to exposure to objective hazards, like falling rock or ice, or literal exposure to cold and bad weather. In both cases the result is failure to achieve the objective, to do the climb.

Leading implies limits to protection. You have to make choices, but how do you decide what to do and when to do it? Start with our safe-equals-simple rule: take the easiest way out when it comes to protection. It's easy and fast to place runners on horns or trees; if they are sound, don't bother with placing nuts. Carefully check the edges of horns and chockstones. Are they sharp enough to cut a runner? Is the rock so rotten that the edges may crumble and the runner fail? Will the whole damn thing break off and clobber the belayer? If your evaluation shows that, say, the chickenhead is marginal, use it only when you really need the marginal increase in protection.

Rule number 2: you should have good protection wherever you are absolutely terrified of falling. On your first lead, the entire pitch may fit this description, but soon experience will allow you to judge the difficulty and anticipate where you need protection. A huge roof is a good sign; so is a blank wall. Learn to examine a stretch of rock and imagine how you will climb it: where you can stand comfortably, where you can rest, what you can reach, where you will place the next piece of protection.

The great Joe Brown climbed so well because he could visualize very precisely where his body would fit on a rock face. Though not especially strong, Brown was able to ration his strength carefully by ingenious placement of his body. This ability to visualize, to climb a route mentally before making a single move, was what made him great. It allowed him to climb where better athletes fell.

Look ahead, then, and protect *before* difficulties.

Less obvious is that you should protect with strong, secure runners early in the pitch. Falling on a short length of rope means there is less rope to absorb impact force. The runners must withstand that impact. Think about using a shock-absorbing runner on your first piece.

Remember, too, that longer falls put the belay chain under stress for a longer time, and thus they increase the likelihood of failure of some link. So also consider using larger nuts early in the pitch. The larger chock may be better able to hold the higher forces of a fall early in the lead, and meanwhile, you won't have to lug the extra weight. Obviously, you don't use a big chock just to get rid of it when you see a long stretch of big crack looming ahead. But you can play a mental game of selecting the biggest piece that you can get in *here* while leaving yourself enough gear to protect yourself up *there*.

Another rule: you want protection right at the beginning of a climb to aim the belay or to avoid the levering action of rope drag on subsequent pieces. A nut slotted upward at the start of a vertical crack will secure higher nuts slotted for a downward pull. On the other hand, you may want to forgo protection right before a traverse or a bulge if it will cause severe rope drag in the pitch. In that case it is better to protect during a traverse than right at the start. If a vertical section follows the traverse, don't put a piece right at the end of the traverse — it will force the rope to run at a right angle, creating horrible drag. Instead, place protection a few moves up the vertical section, to smooth out the running rope. Use extra runners to accomplish this if your choice of placements is limited.

How long should a runner be? Well, how far do you want to fall? But that's only one way to look at it. The answer is a little more complicated: a runner should be long enough to minimize rope drag. And what may appear long enough at eyeball level may look very different after you pass an overhang or go around a corner. There was a classic climb at Seneca where a good fixed pin (it's now gone) was placed just under an overhang. It looked so simple: clip the pin, add a 6-foot runner, and clip into the rope. Everybody did it. Then they climbed through the overhang and found the rope jammed between the carabiner and the lip of the roof. Put a second, heavier carabiner on the runner and the move was a breeze.

Climbing is hard enough without rope drag pulling the leader down. Every leader has done at least one climb where something went wrong and he ended up in a tug-of-war with his own rope. Learning to anticipate the position of the rope as you move higher can avoid some of these annoying, even frightening moments. Look at the remainder of the pitch. Try to imagine how the rope's position will change as you make the moves higher up. Could the runner slip into a crack as it is tugged upward? A jam shortens the runner drastically, and its range of motion becomes curtailed in ways that you may not have anticipated. It could become wedged behind a loose block, for example.

I once led a tricky climb straight up a buttress, which finished with an exit on the right side near the top. As I turned that corner to finish, I left two long runners and enjoyed little drag as I reached the belay stance. My second began climbing, repeating my moves. The rope was now moving back and forth on this buttress, with a fairly snug belay from above. Somehow, the tension of the rope caused it to inch up. It crept up the corner, above the last two runners, and worked its way into a crack behind a series of loose blocks. It got harder and harder to take in rope, and finally the rope jammed. The second had to duck under an overhang while I pulled hard enough on the rope to dislodge the blocks. The route was overhanging, so the blocks dropped outward into space, hitting only the scree far below. Still, it was terrifying for the second. He had to watch as several hundred pounds of rock whooshed through the air right

LEFT: How not to clip in. The rope drag will be ferocious, and a fall caught by higher protection could saw the rope on the overhang. RIGHT: Adding a runner helps a lot.

ROCK SPORT

behind his head, then smashed into bits and sent the dust wafting upward, bringing with it that acrid, evil, brimstone smell. And then the poor guy had to finish the climb.

So consider not only what your upcoming moves will do to the runner, but also how the second's moves will affect it: quite different things may happen.

Belays

As the second, you should minimize the time you take to break down the belay and get moving. The gear should be reracked in something resembling the leader's style, so that he doesn't have to spend time hunting for the right piece on the next belay.

Dropped gear is a bummer. It is often best to first remove a nut from the rock, then unclip it from the rope and rack it. If the piece is at an awkward spot and removal is difficult, you might want to unclip and rack any extra runners and carabiners, then reclip the troublesome piece into the rope before you begin working on it in earnest.

You're leading? When the second arrives at the belay stance, have his anchor ready. Tell him precisely where to clip in. It may be a good idea to describe the anchors, especially if you haven't climbed together before.

A nondirectional bombproof belay is best, since it allows you to start the next pitch immediately. (Review the quick equalizations techniques illustrated in Chapter 3.) In the real world, you may have to settle for security from downward pulls while bringing up the second, then use the gear retrieved to complete a good anchor for the next pitch.

When you reach a belay stance, look for some kind of anchor in place — a chock stone, a bush, a piton — and quickly secure yourself to this. Then you can tell the belayer he is off belay. He can now prepare to climb — tighten up his shoes, chalk up, pray to various deities. He can remove some points of the belay while taking care to remain clipped into at least one secure point until he is told he is on belay. His anchor need no longer be strong enough to hold a leader fall, only body weight.

Meanwhile you, the leader, already secured to one point, complete the belay anchor. If you have limited hardware, you would place pieces for downward pull. Protection for upward pull could be placed later and equalized in opposition to the existing points to make a nondirectional anchor for the next lead. Thorough familiarity with these techniques can make this process flow effortlessly. The consequences of a screwup can be embarrassing, at best.

I know a guide who, upon reaching a large ledge, told his client he was off belay. He was hunting around for chock placements when he suddenly found himself being pulled backwards, off the ledge. After hurtling through space, he was caught by the rope some distance below his last runner. The client had unclipped from his belay and fallen off his stance while trying to remove one of the anchor points. Guide and client were both caught by that last runner and left dangling off the cliff.

Each climber should have been clipped into an anchor point.

The real tactic for lead climbing is efficiency. Whether we're talking runners, chocks, or muscles, the most effective use of resources is the key to success. Crag climbs are the place to hone your skills. Once the techniques are second nature, you can apply them to alpine routes, where they are the margin between success and failure, if not safety and peril.

6

DESCENT

A good portion of the climbing day is taken up with getting down. The simplest solution is to walk off an easy descent route. This involves only a bit of route finding. When the route gets steep, you downclimb. Face outward on easy ground, sideways when it gets a bit harder or traverses. When there is any difficulty, however, you have to face in, and here lies the problem: climbing down is much harder than climbing up because it is more difficult to see your next footholds.

Downclimbing is an art that has to be practiced, and the time to practice it is when you're on a top rope. You don't want to learn the value of this skill the hard way. Every climber, no matter how skilled, has to back off some moves, if only to rest and work them out. So downclimbing is a vital part of safe lead climbing. Don't get into something that you can't get out of. When top roping, I try to downclimb as close to the limit of my abilities as my strength will allow.

Straighten your arms, with hands at chest height, so that you can lean outward and examine the rock below you. You may need to bend one knee, and lean sideways to see down from the side rather than straight down. From this position you should be able to judge the size and shape of the holds below.

As a last resort, rappel. This is the most dangerous maneuver in mountaineering because you are totally committed to the rope and the anchor. Here again, rope handling is the key to speed and safety. Any alpine climb will require two ropes. This is simply a prudent precaution against damage to the climbing rope and it greatly reduces descent time. Double 9mm ropes are most useful in such situations. If you are climbing with an 11mm, consider taking along a 9mm as a haul line, or at least trail it. If a 9mm is beyond your means, one 7mm will do. At least half of the time you will be pulling down on the heavier rope, therefore pulling up on the lighter line. (When you are descending from a long day's climb, you can tell the difference.) Use the double fisherman's knot to tie together two ropes of different sizes for rappels.

Avoid the bounding, Hollywood-style rappels. Each jump shock-loads the anchor as well as your rappelling device. Carabiners have been known to fail under such loads. The rappel brake, no matter what kind of device you are using, will heat up, and the heat can damage the rope. Lastly, such jumping around is most likely to dislodge loose rocks that can imperil others in the party as well as damage the remainder of the rope below you.

Every year a number of climbers simply rappel off the end of their ropes. Using a Prusik safety and tying the ends of the rope together can prevent this from happening. Do not use Kevlar cord as a Prusik.

When starting a rappel, avoid dragging the ropes across the edge of the rock, such as the edge of the ledge you are leaving. During the rappel, avoid any side-to-side motion, which can saw the rope back and forth over any edges near the anchor. When the rope is weighted, as in a rappel, it is much more subject to cutting. Needless to say, cutting your rope while you are hanging on it is not a good idea.

When rigging rappels with a single rope, place the rope so that

Figure 8 rappel with Prusik safety. Keep your hand cupped around the knot so that it will slide easily. The brake hand would be on the right side in this picture.

the anchor (tree, horn, sling, whatever) is a few feet to the side of the middle marker (you do have the middle of your rope marked, don't you?). Pull down on the side with the middle marker below the anchor. Repeat the process at the next rappel, but put the middle marker on the other side of the anchor so that you have some chance of distributing the wear on your rope. With two ropes, remember which side of the anchor the knot is on and pull down that side.

The figure 8 locked off. The active end of the rope was pulled left till it jammed between the standing end and the ring. This is a lot more secure than it looks.

Always check the pull-down before the last member of the party rappels so that you don't have to climb back up to fix it. Consider carrying one or more descending rings, which decrease the likelihood that the rappel will get stuck. Each ring weighs about an ounce and costs about a buck but can be worth its weight in gold. A ring can mean a safe retreat in midpitch and saves a lot of wear and tear on the rope—and on the climbers who have to pull it down. Unlike a rappel sling, a ring is strong enough to reuse. If the hollow rolled-aluminum rings made by SMC make you nervous, there are solid rings.

What should you do when you hang up a rappel line? The first choice, on easy ground, is to go back up the rope, hand over hand. You can tie one Prusik around both ropes and slide it up as you climb. This will also work for climbing the rock back up to the anchor, or at least to the snag. If the wall is unclimbable, then use two Prusiks and ascend the doubled rope.

But before doing any of these maneuvers, tie off the ends of the rope. Tie the ends together, then anchor them. If one end of the rope is out of reach, remember that logically, there has to be enough rope on your end to enable you to reach the other end. Tie into the end you have and climb up to the other end. You can be belayed and even place runners while climbing up. As a last choice, prusik up the single line, but place runners and stay on belay because you are suspended from the jam. If it pops, you will need the runners to catch your fall. Your partner belays with the end of the rope you had, and the Prusiks are your attachment to the rope. Scary stuff, to be avoided at all costs.

Falling

The era of "The leader must not fall" is long gone. If you climb long enough, you will fall. So there are two rules about falling: first, don't fall, and second, don't be totally unprepared to fall. Beyond this there are two considerations, safety and ethics.

Falling is getting safer, but it will never be totally safe. By definition you are out of control when falling, and climbers are the ultimate control freaks. You can maintain some measure of control, however, by planning for a fall. You know where the crux is, so you protect for it, and your protection works as anticipated. Even on a new or unknown route, you will know from experience when moves are getting difficult. Since you are mentally climbing at least one move ahead, you can anticipate difficulty, or moves that you may not be able to reverse.

There are also those unpredictable falls, where holds break or turn out to be wet or iced up, and you are gone before you know it.

More often, there are fractions of a second when you realize you are going to fall. The one thing to remember is to let go. A lot of arm and hand injuries occur when the leader, turned faller, panics as both feet and one hand lose their grip and he tries to hang on with one inadequate handhold. Suddenly body weight and momentum wrench it loose. The effect on joints and ligaments can be as devastating as grounding out. A deathlike grip on a hold can be much more damaging than a finger or hand jam, since all tissues are in active use.

The farther you fall, really, the easier it is. A fall with a lot of rope out will be caught much more gently than a fall near the belay point, as there is more rope to stretch and absorb impact. Those are the falls that seem to last forever — you may not even feel any impact at all, just notice that you've stopped falling.

Try to anticipate the direction of your fall. You will drop straight out of an overhang but will pendulum back in the direction of your top piece as the rope catches you. Time seems to expand while you are airborne, allowing you to make some adjustments in your position. Clearing your feet quickly of the surrounding rock will allow you to remain upright. No harness can guarantee this. Having your feet clear and poised for impact can help. Knees should be flexed, toes pointed slightly down so that the impact will go from the ball of the foot, back to the heel, then to the ankle, and finally up to the big bones of the thigh. (That's the PLF, parachute landing fall, for you skydivers.) Finish with a roll to the side in case of a ground fall. Whatever else you do, close your mouth; one of the messiest falls I ever saw was a guy who just about bit his tongue off. He wasn't badly hurt otherwise, but he nearly drowned before getting back to the ledge of his last belay stance.

Hitting the ground or a ledge is the worst fall. If you hit feet first, try to grab something so that you don't roll off the ledge or down the slope. Tumbling through scree often does far greater harm than hitting the ground. You may lose some flesh grabbing at rocks and trees but that may be better than bouncing your brains down a scree slope that was a Class 2 walk-up an hour ago. Being a broken body in the middle of the trail is damned embarrassing. Everyone keeps asking, "What happened?" Well, what the hell do you *think* happened?

If you are in a corner, you know you are going to drop down the corner and swing back into it when you are caught by the protection. You should look for projections on either wall, things you may hit on the way down. Push off to avoid them. You may want to have arms out in front of you to absorb the impact of the swing back into the corner. Watch your knees: it may be better to have your legs straight up and down than to be banging your kneecaps. Try to stay facing into the corner; if you land with your back to it, you can't break the fall and you are most likely to hit the back of your head—always a serious proposition.

Don't hesitate to yelp, squeal, or swear, any of which will alert the belayer to your imminent (or present) fall. In a perfect world the belayer would always be at maximum readiness to catch a fall, but this world isn't perfect. Warned, the belayer can make subtle adjustments in stance that will soften the impact on him and minimize the amount of stretch that will come out of the anchors and climbing rope. That stretch increases the distance that you will fall, thereby increasing the chance you will hit something.

The ethics of falling is a slippery subject in itself. There are those who contend that any fall taints a climb, just like hanging on protection. True enough, but it implies that a climber should never be at his limit. Never falling may be desirable—it is certainly better style—but fear of falling may arrest your development as a climber. The ability to recognize your limit on any particular day is something that comes with experience. Some people always push the limit and fall; some climb right at their limit, upping their standards climb by climb; others back off and progress only by fits and starts, going through the doldrums when it seems they will never get better. Climbers can go through periods that fit each description: spasmodic progress through 5.8; climbing at the limit on 5.9 and easy 5.10; taking repeated falls on extreme climbs. While they might be said to be climbing in better style on the easier climbs, that doesn't mean that it might not be right for them to attempt the harder ones.

We now enter the fuzziest realm of climbing—the Head Trip. It may have become obvious that climbing is a whole lot more mental than it looks. You can test grip strength, endurance, and balance, but there is no precise measure of the condition of the organ between your ears. You can't just go down to the gym and work on it.

Some people have the ability to climb to their full potential. It's a gift—they suspend doubt and go. The rest of us suffer and agonize as our fear gnaws away at our confidence. Some days the fear wins: you back off if you are lucky, or fall if your luck runs out. You can't fake it. The climb is not impressed by how successful you are at the office, who your daddy is, where you went to school, how hard you trained for this, or how bad you want it. No—if you can't climb it today, nothing is going to get you by, nothing is going to make you look like you could. Out on the sharp end you are going to meet somebody that you rarely see in your everyday life. Sometimes the encounter is humiliating; the only consolation is that you can come back and it doesn't have to be the same. At other times the person you find out there may surprise you: the realm of the possible gets pushed back and its boundaries expand, never to shrink again.

One important thing to remember is that you can successfully climb forever without all this nonsense. If you want to do comfortable climbs and enjoy your surroundings, your experience is every bit as valid and worthwhile as that of the hardmen. Even if you top-rope forever, it sure beats the hell out of golf.

EQUIPMENT

Climbers have rightly been considered gear freaks. Nobody ever got hurt because a tennis racket wasn't properly strung, but if your climbing gear doesn't do what you want, you are in big trouble. The right equipment can make a difference, if only in your level of confidence. The time you spend selecting your gear and experimenting with it will pay off in peace of mind on the crag.

Rope

Modern rope is 150 or 165 feet of nylon kernmantle (German for core and sheath). Single ropes vary from 10mm to 12mm in diameter; double ropes are 8mm to 9mm.

There are many variables in producing a climbing rope. The ideal rope would have all of the following characteristics: low impact force, low elongation under both impact force and low load, good handling qualities, light weight, water resistance, high ratings for holding falls, resistance to cutting, resistance to abrasion, and (not least) low price.

Climbers must ask themselves what combination of these qualities will be best for their use. There are no really bad ropes, and no rope is much closer to the ideal than any other.

The two largest manufacturers are Edelweiss and Edelrid. Edelweiss ropes are made in Austria. Edelrid ropes are made in West Germany (Edelrid also produced Robbins ropes and Plymouth Goldmantle).

The constructions of the ropes differ, and the resulting difference in the end product is a matter of preference. Edelrid ropes are softer and more flexible, while the Edelweiss are a bit stiffer. Both companies produce a whole range of ropes, all of which are excellent, and none of which are cheap.

Edelweiss ropes are given a water-repellent treatment; the treatment costs extra with Edelrid. Resistance to water is obviously very useful for winter climbing, but it is also good for a rock-climbing rope, since a dry rope is much stronger than a saturated one.

Edelrid offers several ropes with diameters over 11mm; their very size lessens the risk that they will be cut in a fall. The company makes an 8mm rope, which (unlike 9mm ropes) must be used with two strands clipped into each protection point. Ropes used this way are called twin ropes. Edelweiss is making a single 10mm rope that is especially resistant to cutting.

Mammut ropes are produced in Switzerland and distributed in the United States by Seattle Manufacturing Corporation (SMC). If the price is right, they are a good deal. There was some criticism of fast wear on Mammut ropes, but I have seen no evidence of this. Mammut used to make the Chouinard ropes. They were very highly regarded for their long-wearing sheaths and ability to absorb the impact force of short falls without adding a lot of stretch to a long fall. With the 10.2 and 10.5, Chouinard pioneered the idea of a safe single rope smaller than 11mm in diameter.

Beal ropes handle like Edelrids, but the specifications are more like Edelweiss. They have the reputation of fuzzing up rapidly. There is nothing wrong with this per se, but it defeats the purpose of any dry coating, and the rope drags more through protection. The Chouinard ropes made by Beal are less prone to this but show wear faster than the Chouinard 10.5mm made by Mammut. Beal makes ropes in 8.8mm, 10.5mm, and 11mm sizes. Joanny ropes, made in France, tend to fuzz up, as do Elite Bernina ropes. Interalp ropes are very soft, almost limp. There is a dry version.

Goldmantle was made by Edelrid with all the specs of an Edelrid Classic except for greater low-load elongation, which makes it a poor choice for top roping. If you buy a used Goldmantle for leading, ask whether it was used for top roping; the top roping may have twisted the sheath away from the core and put in some terrific kinks. A beginner who wants a cheap rope for top roping is best off using a nonstretch 9mm and then spending money on a good lead rope when the time comes. The 9mm can also be used for hauling and rappelling.

At long last there are American-made ropes. The 11mm, 10-fall Maxim is made by New England Ropes. There were returns of early Maxims with lumpy spots. Apparently there is no real structural damage, but the rope is also comparatively heavy. The other domestic manufacturer, Bluewater, makes 9mm and 11mm ropes, and dry is an option. They perform as well as the best of the European ropes.

Perlon for slings and chock cords should not be limp. Edelweiss Power Rope and Chouinard Cord are somewhat stiff, allowing better control when you manipulate the chock without the lever action of the wire. You end up using both in order to color-code chocks. In equivalent diameters, Chouinard Cord gets into nuts easier. Edelweiss seems to run a bit thicker. The usual solution is to put Chouinard in the smaller nuts using a given size cord and Edelweiss in the larger ones. Bluewater makes accessory cord, and Kevlar and Spectra cords offer strong, lightweight alternatives.

What about using two 9mm ropes instead of a single 11mm? On sea cliffs, some sharp types of rocks, and in the mountains, it is often a good idea. In alpine climbing, in fact, you simply cannot set out with just one rope. Double 9mm ropes are very good for ice climbing; all those sharp objects are going to eat a rope sooner or later. A 7mm line, kept in the pack for rappels, is useful because it gives you a rope to pull down that isn't frozen stiff. You could use a

10.5mm to climb and save the 9mm for hauling, rappelling, and the traverse pitch that comes up now and then. Some rock climbers like double 9s for extreme routes because it can be easier to clip in a rope that only goes through alternate pieces. When trying to make a desperate clip, they like the feeling that the slack they are pulling out is not extra distance they are going to fall.

The chief thing to remember in double roping is not to get the two ropes twisted. This is nowhere near so easy as it sounds. It requires conscious and continuous effort on the part of both the leader and the belayer. If the ropes are crossed too much, they can jam hopelessly. At a minimum, the advantages of using two ropes will be lost.

A 300-foot 9mm rope will have two 150-foot sections of distinctly different colors: one light and one dark. The idea is to be able to tell the halves apart even in fading light. If you buy two 150-foot ropes, select the colors with this in mind. As you are climbing, you may need to call for slack; you can identify the right rope by color, and you want your second to be able to tell the difference, too.

When you're belaying, you can use the 9–11mm Sticht plate for two 9mm ropes — it will work as well as a double 9mm plate. You must be absolutely sure that the ropes are not twisted as you let them out. Clip one rope to a carabiner above the Sticht plate and attach it to the harness. This prevents twisting right at the plate. With a body belay, use the same technique and keep the index finger of the nonbrake hand between the ropes. The leader will employ a series of calls to specify which rope he is manipulating: "Runner on red," he may yell, or "Slack on yellow." The call "runner on" has nothing to do with baseball, by the way, and it is quite useful even with a single rope because it lets the belayer know that the leader was tugging on the rope only to get enough slack to clip in, not to make some mad dash up the rock, requiring continuous feed of slack.

Although double roping is not as useful as most Europeans think, it is not as difficult as most Americans imagine. Needless to say, it is best to practice a bit on easy climbs until you master the technique.

When should you retire your rope? Beyond certain obvious criteria, there is no nice, neat answer. The obvious first:

• If the sheath is cut so that you can see through to the core, retire the rope. The sheath provides some of the total strength of the rope. If it is cut anywhere, the rope is useless, even for top roping.

• If you have reached the number of leader falls your rope is rated for, retire it. The U.I.A.A. (Union Internationale des Associations d'Alpinisme) rates ropes for the minimum number of their test falls that samples held. Fall factors range from 0 to 2 and are defined as the distance fallen divided by the length of rope paid out by the belayer.

• If there is any evidence of core damage or severed internal strands, retire the rope. Put the rope under slight tension to examine it more effectively. Look for any area that is thinner or feels mushy or lumpy. These are signs that the internal strands have been severed and rearranged by some impact. Ropes will have a slight compression, a bit of flattening, after a hard fall. You might want to mark the spot and check it again the next day. In the absence of sheath damage or detectable core irregularities, you can continue to use the rope.

Now the criteria that are a little more vague:

• Sheath abrasion is a concern for many climbers. Softer ropes do fuzz up more than others, but there is no real relation to strength. Use a magnifier to examine a sample of strands. If 50 percent of the filaments in the strands are cut, it is time to retire the rope from lead climbing. Assuming there has not been any damage from falls, such a rope can be used for top roping, rappelling, or hauling until the core shows through.

• A rope is probably good for at least two seasons. After that its handling qualities will tell you something about its condition. If it kinks badly, the sheath has separated from the core. This is not terminal, but it indicates that the rope has done some hard work. Examine the sheath foot by foot, check a sample of the strands, and come to a decision.

Rope should be washed to remove grit and aluminum oxide, which cut the small fibers, fuzzing up the rope and making it fatter, more likely to jam or drag through carabiners or take on water and freeze into something resembling a steel cable. There is a controversy, however, over how it should be washed and with what.

There is no doubt that rinsing a rope in cool water will remove a lot of surface particles and cannot possibly damage a rope. Mammut and MSR report that their ropes can be washed in water up to 120 degrees F with soap or nylon-safe detergent (like Woolite) in a home washing machine. Edelrid specified 86 degrees F and sanctioned the use of the washing machine, including the spin cycle. Edelweiss considers the use of a washing machine dangerous.

If you are going to use a washing machine, make sure it has a central spindle-type agitator, not a plunger type. Special rope washers were designed for caving ropes, but they proved to be a bad idea. They simply blasted crud *into* the core of the rope, doing more harm than good.

To do it by hand, first rinse the rope. If it still looks dirty, slosh it around with some Woolite, then rinse it again.

The rope will air-dry pretty easily if hung on a line or a rack. You can also drag it across the lawn (not your average city park, please). Store the rope out of sunlight, but not in an attic or closet that tends to get uncomfortably hot.

Remember, a rope is a tool. It has complex parts that perform physical work to absorb the energy of falling and supporting weight under tension. On every climb or rappel the thousands of tiny filaments in the core and the sheath are stretching and recoiling in response to those forces. The rope works best when it is allowed to recover, to reassume its position of rest. Letting the rope hang free for its entire length will speed up the process as well as help you avoid snags. Attach a quart bottle of water (2 pounds), clipped into a smooth figure-eight knot, to let the rope lower nicely, so that it won't hang up when retrieved. You may see the bottle spinning around at the end of the rope as accumulated kinks come out. Pull the rope back up, taking care not to drag the whole thing over an edge. Let it lie for a while, then coil it without forcing the coils (don't, for example, wrap it between feet and knees). I coil by dropping the rope over my head, around the neck, making each coil down

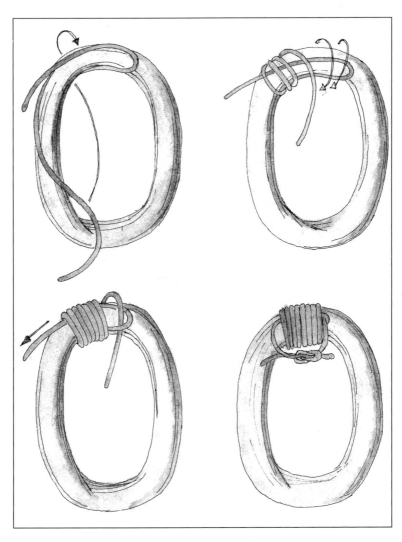

Coiling the rope. Finish the coil by making a U at the working end, then wrapping the standing end four or more times around the coil, working toward the closed end of the U. Feed the standing end up through the U and tighten the working end. You can tie off the ends with a square knot if you like. To uncoil, unwrap the standing end, then feed the rope from the working end; the rope should come free of tangles.

to my waist. This saves my arms. At the end of a long climb, coiling a 7- or 8-pound rope can seem like a lot of work. Repeating the process for multiple rappels can be exhausting.

Top roping makes a rope harder to handle. The falls do not damage the fibers, but the cumulative effect is severe kinking. Any rappel, however, causes wear on the rope. Downclimbing or walking off a climb is often faster than rigging a rappel and will save the rope. Careful use of the rope combined with washing and hanging it out after a hard season can make the rope much easier to work with. These precautions can help you avoid the crisis of a jammed belay.

Runners

The runner, along with the carabiner and the climbing rope, forms the basic chain of protection. It is the lightest, surest, easiest form of protection — and the most overlooked.

Runners are now almost exclusively tubular nylon webbing. Good webbing is continuous weave, with no visible seams on the edges. Standard runners are 6 feet of 1-inch webbing. To make a loop, some people use the water knot, some the double fisherman's knot. The latter, some climbers say, makes the runner easier to handle. The water knot takes about 6 inches less material to tie, but it is not so strong or stable as the double fisherman's knot. I have never seen it untie in tubular webbing, but I have seen it untie in flat webbing and in rope. The ends of the water knot can be taped down to lessen the chance of the knot's untying. But be careful what kind of tape you use on nylon. Troll makes tape specifically for use on nylon. Many climbers use ¾-inch cloth and plastic colored tapes made by Minnesota Mining and Manufacturing (3M), makers of Scotch brand tapes. These appear to have no ill effect on nylon. So you can tape your slings, mark the middle of your rope, and identify climbing equipment without damage. Tape is handy for marking carabiners. You can use two colors — one light band opposite the gate opening, and a darker band opposite the hinge. For carabiners without a blind gate, the bands let you see immediately the location of the gate opening.

Sewn slings are now of good enough quality and reasonable

price to consider. Far and away the best ones are made by Troll. Troll supertape is a light blue, flat, nylon tape, 3mm thick. The ⅝-inch (15mm) is rated at 2,000 kilograms (4,400 pounds), and the 1-inch (25mm) is rated at 2,700 kilograms (6,000 pounds). The German alpine club's tests found that Troll tapes are stronger even than their rated strength. I especially like a double runner of the ⅝-inch. The flat webbing stays around blocks and flakes better than the tubular, and it is much lighter than a 1-inch runner. When carried doubled around the body, it is less cumbersome, too. Troll tapes are not cheap. The Bluewater Spectra runners are the closest American approximation, and they are much stronger.

The Rabbit Runner sewn sling is not as strong as a regular runner and rather expensive. Several manufacturers are now producing similar slings. They consist of a length of webbing with each end sewn into a loop. These loops can be clipped together to come close to the closed loop of the standard runner, but they are still not as strong. A well-sewn loop of webbing gives the strongest possible runner. If you tie a Rabbit Runner with overhand loop knots, make sure that the short end is on the inside of the knot. If tied on the outside, the short end can work through by rubbing on the rock. At least one recent death can be attributed to this error.

If you want to sew your own runners, use #24 polyester thread and make 24 passes over a 4-inch overlap with 10 stitches to the inch. That's for 1-inch webbing runners. For 9/16-inch or ¾-inch, 12 passes will suffice. Use a zigzag pattern, running lengthwise. This pattern was developed years ago at REI (Recreational Equipment Inc.). Others may work quite well, but should be tested. Many commercial sewn runners are constructed by bar tacking; when done carefully, with the proper machine, this is secure. If I were going to sew runners, I think I would copy the Troll pattern of an overlap of 8½ inches with two sewn sections separated by just under 1 inch. This central section can be used for the carabiner that clips the runner to the rope. The finished circumference is a matter of personal preference, but about 4 feet for a single runner and 8 feet for a double would suit most people.

Everybody has gotten into the sewn sling act now. There are

new materials, like strong Spectra Webbing, which is ⅝-inch and 1-inch supertape rated at 6,000 pounds. Consider strength, durability, and price. Buy various colors so that you can tell the slings apart when they are slung around your body.

Several manufacturers are now making special runners designed to absorb impact force by internal seams that break deliberately, giving a dynamic belay. They work but are expensive, and you wouldn't want to use them more than once. They are popular with ice climbers who carry fewer runners, fall less, and really need low impact force on their protection. Some are sewn with bar tacks. As the tacks break to absorb force, carabiner gates can vibrate open. Use locking carabiners with such runners — an open carabiner gate greatly reduces strength, perhaps well below the impact force of the fall.

Chouinard 9/16-inch supertape, when doubled between carabiners for a quick draw, is as strong as 1-inch but a lot lighter and less bulky. Use 5 feet for such a runner and tie the double fisherman's knot. The quickdraw configuration gives you a readily available short runner, as well as a full-length runner, and a ready-made, self-equalizing anchor. The bottom strands are clipped into separate points — wired nuts, for example — and the top carabiner goes to the rope.

This 9/16-inch comes in several colors, so you can color-code your quickdraws as well as your other runners. Different colors make it easier to pick out the right strand from that mess of webbing around your neck, and untangle the runner with a minimum of fuss. There are other advantages, too. Often during a climb, a second may have trouble with a nut and ask how it was put in. It may be hard to see what nut he is working on, but you can see the color of the runner, or he can tell you what the color is. You can then describe how the nut was placed. And with complex belays, it is easier to tell someone, "Clip into the blue sling" than "Clip into that sling . . . no, not *that* one, the *other* one!" This lesson comes from big wall climbing, where belay stations are often a mess of runners. Seeing your belayer clip himself into an anchor you intended for just the haul bag is not good.

Chouinard also makes an excellent ½-inch webbing that is lighter and stronger than other brands of ⁹⁄₁₆-inch. It is very useful in 2-foot runners, girth-hitched to the racking sling, for tying off small flakes and threading into the eyes of old fixed pitons.

Half-length runners, 3 feet of ⁹⁄₁₆-inch, are useful for this same purpose, as well as providing security for wired nuts on very hard climbs. You want a runner to keep the nuts in or connect a nest of marginal placements, but you just don't want to fall any farther than you have to. Like the ½-inch, these half-length runners can be girth-hitched to the rack.

Flat 1-inch webbing can also be used in runners. It is lighter and cheaper and seems to wear better than tubular, but it is not quite as strong. It is most useful as a long runner, to be thrown around trees or large blocks. Flat webbing is less likely to creep off knobs or out of flakes. Some flat webbing intended for harness and étriers is too stiff for use in runners.

How many runners should you carry? Well, it can't hurt to have several small runners of ½-inch and ⁹⁄₁₆-inch, two 5-foot quickdraws of ⁹⁄₁₆-inch, and eight 6-foot runners of 1-inch, all tubular. Consider one 10-foot double runner of cheaper white 1-inch tubular or 1-inch flat. Once you start to second climbs, you should always have enough runners and carabiners to set up one belay and clip yourself in anywhere. Beginners and mountaineers will find they use more runners and need longer ones. Extreme rock climbs require fewer and smaller runners.

Carabiners

The present state of the art leaves one manufacturer far ahead of the rest: Chouinard. His carabiners are cheaper, stronger, individually stress-tested, and inspected for gate action and workmanship.

Chouinard's standard carabiner was the product that allowed him to dominate the market. When Robbins introduced a Salewa-produced tubular oval, it was a must for the big-wall climber. With a production line in the United States, Chouinard was able to turn out a slightly stronger tubular at a cheaper price. Salewa tubular

D-shaped carabiners are much stronger (2,000kg) and very roomy. They are quite good for free climbing uses but they are very expensive in the United States.

In the 1970s SMC produced the Ultimate Oval, the strongest oval up to that time. SMC tested batches of carabiners and generally upgraded the quality of their workmanship, on both the oval and the traditional D. Chouinard simply designed a stronger oval and offered it at a cheaper price. The Bonaiti Ultralight, an offset D shape in thin rod stock, was very popular at the Shawangunks due to its light weight, cheap price, and thin gate notch, which allowed easy entry into old fixed pins and bolt hangers (the blind gates on Chouinard's and SMC's were too big). Some Bonaitis, however, had problems. Gates were too stiff (some used to catch your thumb before you could get it out of the way) or opened too easily. The rate of returns of these carabiners to climbing shops began to climb sharply, along with the price. Chouinard introduced his Light D, of somewhat similar construction, but better quality. He also began stress-testing each individual carabiner, while increasing the price 25 cents to cover the added step.

The blind gates are a bit thinner now, but clipping into old hardware is still awkward. If you can find a couple of good Bonaiti Ultralights, keep them: they come in handy. Clog 10mm offset Ds are stronger and have a nicer gate action. They can get into most hardware, but they are expensive. Chouinard came up with a carabiner of similar design, the Quicksilver, with a large gate opening but thin gate catch, to get into bolts or pins; it has bombproof strength.

An oval carabiner can be a real advantage, since it may be easier to turn over, so that the gate is opening down and out, after you've clipped into an awkwardly placed fixed pin. The offset D carabiner may get in, but it is hard to turn it over to the safer position. Some offsets are designed to be okay with the gate opening up.

New ridgeless ovals and Ds are being produced in the United States and distributed by several equipment wholesalers. They are heavier yet weaker than some of the old SMCs. In early batches, the gates did not close flush, leaving the sharp interior edges of the gate prongs to abrade ropes. Newer lots of these carabiners show better workmanship and have stronger ratings, and they are somewhat less expensive than other carabiners.

Chouinard retooled his carabiner line in 1985 to produce models that were cheaper, lighter, and stronger. The only drawback is that he let his prices creep up again.

Lightweight, small D carabiners for free climbing are very popular. SMC and Chouinard have entries, but DMM and Wild Country (both made by Denny Morehouse) are the lightest. Too small to be used with 1-inch webbing, they would be impossible in winter, always clamped around a mittened thumb, since their gates are very stiff. T section 'biners, coated gates, and fancy locking collars add to the array. Avoid carabiners with dogleg gates and any 'biner made in France, where gear isn't always tested. Omega Pacific makes a light D that is cheap, has great gate action, and shows fine workmanship.

Locked up. Screwgate (locking) carabiners are used with some harnesses, rappelling, and belaying devices. They can lighten the hardware load, since they can replace two standard carabiners. But they are heavier than regular models, 'biner for 'biner, and their collars are subject to jamming from wear and tear, dirt, or improper use. They will jam hopelessly if screwed down while the 'biner is holding weight. Cavers, who need the security for their rappelling and prusiking, often carry pliers for jammed collars. For all the difficulty they can cause, the screw collars often don't do the job they were intended to do. Most are round, or nearly round, and friction on a rock surface or a running rope can open them right up.

Clog screwgates are super strong and fairly reliable. The newest models have improved collars to decrease jams. They are very large, and useful on a big wall, where multiple ropes and runners are being clipped in. The bottom of the inside of the Clog D is nicely rounded to avoid lurches in étriers. This is also a good design for use of the Munter hitch belay, since this knot tends to jam in Ds.

Salewa and Stubai make screwgates that are very strong, very heavy, and cost a fortune. SMC locking D carabiners are smaller and less expensive than the imports. The current model is reliable, but older designs were less satisfactory. Look for a collar that is removable to facilitate cleaning of the threads. The collar on the older model, which has no visible threads and no removable collar, would jam on a retaining pin if it was subjected to any side load. If you have one of these carabiners and it jams, you can sometimes reverse the process by hand. Try to unscrew the collar while exerting some sideways pressure right where it is jammed on the pin.

Chouinard screwgates have the collar locking on the hinge end of the gate. Jamming is eliminated and the stainless steel collars will take a lot of punishment. Be a bit more careful about screwing them shut because the collars need to travel only a couple of turns to open.

How to unjam a stuck screwgate collar? First, get the carabiner to hold weight. (This is usually the source of the problem. Someone starting a rappel makes a last-second check of the screw collar, not realizing that he has already put weight on the rope. By the end of the rappel, the collar is jammed.) Take in just enough rope to hang on the rappel again and loosen the collar. If this doesn't work, carefully examine the collar for flat spots. Apply pressure on the collar opposite the flat spot, and the collar may start to move. Look for pieces of grit inside the collar, clean the edges of the collar as best you can, and listen for the grinding sound of grit in the internal threads. Water poured into the collar may flush this junk out.

Some 'biners from England come with interesting locking mechanisms that appear less prone to malfunction and much easier to use. Most manufacturers have introduced large screwgate carabiners for use with the Munter hitch belay. The Munter works fairly well on all of them, but it is still awkward to reverse the knot to take in rope. On difficult rock climbs, where the leader may advance to place protection or try the moves, then retreat to rest, the Munter is a real hassle.

Some people solve the problems of screwgates by using quicklinks or Norselinks from yachting suppliers. These are very strong but heavy and expensive. MSR makes an alloy locklink that has none of these disadvantages. It is rated at about 5,000 pounds, which is just strong enough for the bombproof performance expected. Its rounded bottom is also good for the Munter hitch, and its faceted collar cannot be opened by a running rope. The locklink is the safest tool for a military-style carabiner wrap rappel. Do the carabiner wrap with the standing end, or the rope will hop over onto the gate. The advantage of the locklink is that the collar is being rotated shut by the rope. The disadvantage to the locklink or a Norselink is that you have to be sure the collar is closed, since there is no gate. It is hard not to think of it as working like a carabiner.

When you buy any carabiner, look it over carefully. Surface imperfections in forged 'biners may be of no significance, but check the gate action to make sure it opens and closes as easily or stiffly as you like. Look carefully at the sides of the gate catch and the inside of the notch. Marks of friction at certain points will be obvious. Put the carabiner close to your ear and close the gate slowly. The scraping of ill-fitting parts can be heard. All carabiners will develop such problems with use, and they can be corrected, but why buy a brand-new one that isn't perfect?

Never use oil on carabiners in an attempt to get the gates to work better. If an old carabiner has a difficult gate, discard it. The gates work with a spring, and if that is the source of the trouble, nothing will make the 'biner safe again.

A sticky gate can be caused by a burr on the gate of the latch. The burr can be filed off.

Over time the gate may start closing off center. Put the carabiner in a vise and put pressure on the body (not the gate) in the right direction to correct the problem. You can do this by hand in the field, and it often works well enough. But never bend the gate.

Store hardware in a dry place. All aluminum will oxidize a bit; this is the black stuff on your hands and rope. If your gear is outdoors on a long climbing trip, it may develop more noticeable spots of corrosion from dampness. These can be gently sanded off. Anodized carabiners look shiny for a longer time, but they are quite expensive. If you are a sea cliff climber, use fresh water to rinse any equipment exposed to salt spray. Then dry it off.

Chocks

Chocks, or nuts, fall into two basic categories: wedges and cams, both of which can be either active or passive. Active nuts use springs and moving parts to change configuration and grip the rock; passive nuts do not.

Wedges are inherently more secure in most placements but are less versatile and heavier. The question is not which to use but what mix of the two.

Wedges. Clearly, below a certain size only wired wedges are effective. When to switch to cord or webbing is a personal choice that should be dictated by a careful analysis of climbing style and rock qualities.

Either wires are soldered into the wedges or a loop is run through central holes and swaged. In the smallest sizes, soldering is preferable, since the top of cable loop would be too weak.

The first soldered nuts were RPs, shallow, soft brass wedges with a 7-degree taper to maximize surface contact and avoid shearing. The longer side of each nut is equal to the shortest side of the next largest size. HBs, from Wild Country, are somewhat similar but stronger. They make regular and offset wedges for flaring cracks. Chouinard uses steel for soldered nuts to maximize strength, ease removal from placements, and minimize shearing. Soldered cables are stiff and can fray or break if subjected to impact force over edges. So don't use them in horizontal placements, and use runners to avoid crossing the edges of vertical cracks.

The Forrest Arrowhead is a single cable wedge. It is soft copper inside but can be used as a wedge only on its thinnest side. Forrest Copperheads, copper swages on a single wire, can be used as chocks. The single-cable Forrest nuts are less likely to lever out of placements and are known for working in shallow grooves and cracks. Forrest makes a larger wedge, the Foxhead, that is very heavy.

There are at least five vintages of Chouinard stoppers out there. They got lighter and stronger through the years, but the numbers, shapes, and sizes have varied, so know what you are buying. They

What is all this junk? These are wedges and hexes. Better manufacturing technologies allow newer vintages to be lighter and use smaller wires and slings, but the function remains the same.

started out with flat sides, sharp corners, and roughly rectangular shapes; now they are trapezoidal, with flat narrow sides, concave and convex long sides, and rounded edges. Numbers 1 through 3 have straight sides; 1 through 9 come only on wire; 10 through 13 come wired or loose. An earlier experiment with more radical curved sides, intended to cut down on rotation and fit over nubbins, made the nuts too difficult to remove and lessened surface contact.

Rocs have less curve on their narrow profile than stoppers; their wide profile is slightly tapered. Unlike the Chouinards, they are curved in the smaller sizes.

ROCK SPORT

Bluewater makes "classic" flat-sided 6-degree taper wedges. Placed sideways, they are half a size larger.

In larger wedges, the Campbell Saddlewedge and Wedgefast chocks are recommended for use only on their broad sides, not their narrow ends. Their alloys are a bit softer than the Chouinard Stopper, and they can be a bit sticky to recover. They are stronger than the equivalent-sized stoppers because of careful finishing and improvements in the runner pathway. The Saddlewedges use a central groove to avoid rotation of the wedge. All Campbell chocks are anodized with the sizes running in a color-coded spectrum. The Campbells proved popular and are hard to find. Their small Wedgefast chocks were very strong for their size. Some of these were also being made in a narrow width.

DMM Wallnuts continue the central scoop of the Campbell chocks. Numbers 5 through 9 are scooped on two sides, 1 through 4 have only one side scooped, and the number 0 has no scoop. The set runs from under ½ inch to over 1 inch in thickness. The three largest nuts are also available on Spectra cord. Wallnuts are very light and show excellent workmanship.

The mid-'80s saw the introduction of a number of active wedge nuts. They work on the principle of opposed wedges, like stacked stoppers strung on the same perlon loop.

First, there were Sliders, very difficult to place, soft sided, bad in flares or soft rock, but still a favorite. Quickies use small opposing wedges, while Rock N' Rollers use a steel cylinder and soft wedge combination. Quickies are strong, having greater contact area, but they will pivot out of placements. Rollers are more likely to stay in.

The solution for either nut is to use a runner, just like a passive wedge. You can push the small wedge of a Quickie alongside the larger wedge, to stack them sideways. These active wedge chocks make possible protection in pin scars and small, flaring cracks.

Any wired chock can be refined with color-coded shrink tubing around the carabiner end of the cable. This makes it easier to manipulate in a racking 'biner and easier to identify.

Rock N' Roller holds in a rotten, marginal crack. The placement is still somewhat vulnerable to pulling from the side, but it will rotate around the roller without falling out.

       ROCK SPORT

Cams. Lowe Tri-Cams are passive (not spring-loaded) cam nuts. They work better than previous attempts at such a design, but placing them one-handed requires a lot of practice.

SMC made a cam chock that works well, provided you have two hands to place it securely. For parallel-sided granite or desert sandstone cracks, they may offer a cheap alternative to Friends. Clog Cogs and Forrest Titons are also cam chocks. They are very strong, but the area of contact with the rock is small. They tend to hold securely and break the rock quickly.

The other major passive cam is the Chouinard Hexentric. Hexentrics have gone through four design changes over the years. If you are buying used equipment, you may want to look carefully at what you are getting. The earliest hexes were just that, not the eccentric shape of the later models. They offer only three attitudes, and their sizing differs from that of the later models.

The eccentric design made these cams uniquely versatile. Hexes through number 6 have not changed noticeably since. In sizes 7 through 11, weight and strength have been something of a trade-off. The old thick-walled hexes were strong but heavy. They matched the strength of 9mm perlon or 1-inch tubular webbing. Drilled hexes were found to be less strong and could be strung with 8mm. The thin-walled hexes were supposed to be as strong but lighter. Though I have never heard of a hex crushing in a fall, I have seen cord break or cut. Frankly, if you take a fall with enough force to crush a hex, the nut will be the least of your worries. At that kind of impact force, you could get your liver back in the mail with a foreign postmark.

The German alpine club's tests of Chouinard nuts led to some criticism. They claimed the finishing quality on the runner holes was poor, and the holes were not large enough. There is no question that the Ventura factory had some workmanship problems for a time. Sling holes were often not drilled straight. Some even had burr grooves in the sides of the holes, just waiting to eat up a rope. When buying chocks, new or used, look them over carefully. A little work with a file and emery paper can cure most of these deficiencies.

The bottom line was that the larger, thin-walled hexes collapsed before the strength of 9mm was reached. Chouinard now recommends the use of 8mm. This solves one criticism, since the sling holes are much bigger than the 8mm cord (9mm rope was a tight fit). If you are restringing older chocks, you can also use 8mm. In the German tests, 8mm broke at the same strength as 9mm. Tubular webbing can be used to sling hexes. Numbers 5 and up take 1-inch webbing; place the knots on numbers 7 and up inside the nut, so that the sling doesn't interfere with the placement. Hexes 3 and 4 would take 9/16-inch. The 1 and 2 would need 1/2-inch and would not be very strong. Kevlar or Spectra cord can lighten up hexes, and the thin-diameter (5.5mm) makes placements easier.

Some people say a wired hex is a waste; there is no denying that it sacrifices some flexibility. Examine your needs to determine whether hexes 1 through 3 should be wired. Perhaps you do not need the small hexes, perhaps you need them on both wire and perlon or webbing. One compromise is to string numbers 3 and 4 on Spectra and rack them together, while racking wired numbers 1 and 2 together.

Large hexes, numbers 9 and above, can go on 6 feet of webbing and be carried around the body like a runner. You usually want a full-length runner on a nut of that size anyway, and this lightens up the rack a great deal. Kevlar or Spectra would also be a good choice. Spectra is lighter and stronger, but Kevlar is more resistant to cutting.

Many climbers freely admit that they can't figure out how to use hexes. Those are the people they make Friends for, and an increasing number of young climbers, who go from easy climbs to difficult ones in one season, are carrying racks of Friends and wired wedges. That's nice if you can afford the weight and expense, but there comes a time when you simply can't carry enough of that stuff. Any alpine climbing or extreme rock in a remote area will require more versatility in the protection system. The hex is a big-wall chock, born of necessity on the granite of Yosemite. It may pay to learn to work with hexes in crag climbing before you confront something more imposing.

When buying any chocks, new or used, carefully inspect all surfaces. Drilled holes must be straight and smooth, runner holes centered in the chock. Cables should be perfect—no nicks or burrs in any of the strands.

Active cams. Active cam chocks have revolutionized climbing protection. Almost any crack of any shape, from under ½ inch to 5 inches, can easily be protected. The two penalties are weight and cost.

Friends come in cam sizes ½ inch to 4 inches, with half-inch sizes. Technical Friends are narrower, use a cable instead of a central shaft, and come in four sizes, ranging from about ½ inch to 1½ inches. Friends are very versatile but weigh as much as 7 ounces, and the cost is unmentionable.

Contrary to popular belief, it is possible to screw up a Friend placement. As with all cams, get good contact. You must use the right size; too large and the release rod will jam at the back of the shaft, precluding removal; too small and the cams may extend too far, popping the retaining wires and breaking the cam.

Rope drag or tension can cause a Friend to walk back into a crack, out of reach. If it's inserted into a vertical crack, the shaft can be pulled downward while the cams are moving in the crack. The shaft can jam, or the cams can engage so that the retractor bar is locked. Some of these problems arise from the tendency to cram in a Friend, without a runner. Many climbers use a Friend as a sort of top rope. When they get desperate for protection, they "inject a unit." They don't bother to use a runner, as they would with any other type of nut, because the Friend will not come out due to rope drag—it will only work its way in. The result is poor style for the leader and an unholy mess for the second.

A better practice is to treat your Friend like any other nut. Use of a half-length runner or a quickdraw will solve many of the retrieval problems. The Friend is usually rigged with a short piece of 1-inch tubular webbing to keep it from banging around too much on the rack. When used as part of the protection system, this sling should be lengthened with some sort of runner.

The German alpine club's tests found Friends to be bombproof.

Friend. Full contact with the four spring-loaded cams makes for a good placement. The Friend is jammed straight up into a horizontal crack in a roof, with the shaft aligned with the direction of the fall. Upward tugging from the leader would pull the shaft horizontal, pointing the unit straight into the crack. Further vibration would just "walk" it in deeper. Passive nuts could be slotted into such cracks if there were constrictions, but this crack has none, and the walls are slightly flaring. The Friend cannot be overextended, so the placement is sound, but a runner would help avoid rope drag.

A downward-flaring crack would be impossible to protect without the Friend. This #1 Friend is strung with Kevlar cord through the forward holes, for greater efficiency in horizontal cracks.

EQUIPMENT

141

*The Friend will grip in lots of improbable places, like this hollow tree trunk.
The Friend is a #2.*

Either the slings or the rock broke before the Friends even budged. So check your slings, and replace them when they're worn. The manufacturer recommends a 24-inch webbing sling tied with a ring bend to yield a 4-inch-long sling. For horizontal placements, a sling of Kevlar or Spectra cord through the small holes closer to the cams might be an alternative.

As for the Friend itself, an occasional shot of WD40 or LPS 1 will keep it working smoothly. When (not if) a Friend jams, have the leader tie you off so that you can set to work on it. It will require both hands, a couple of tools you probably have, and a lot of luck. The retractor bar can be pulled back with the holes of a nut tool handle (some tools have holes or grooves in the lower shaft designed for Friend retrieval). Often, one side has to be pulled back much farther than the other. If both sides have to be forced back, try using two wired nuts. Slip the cables around the retractor bar. You can even clip these into runners so that you can lean back and pull, using all your strength and body weight (you are tied off, aren't you?). Push on the butt of the shaft at the same time, so that all your force is directed at compressing the cans, not setting the Friend even deeper.

If these heroic measures still don't work, you may have to do a bit of excavating in the crack. Internal flakes and knobs may be the cause of your hangup. It is easier to break these than to pound on the Friend. Working the shaft around may reverse the moves that got the Friend jammed in the first place. (It is pretty hard to visualize what Friends do once they start moving around on their own.) Getting the cams to start moving is the first step. Then try different directions until the retractor bar can do its job.

The ultimate solution to Friends in a jam is to buy and carry another piece of equipment: a special retrieving tool. If you climb a lot with Friends, it's worth the investment: it works like a charm.

Chouinard Camalots are four-cam units, covering a wider range in each size. The cable stems are protected with nylon sleeves, and unlike all other active cam nuts, they are designed to function like passive chocks at full extension.

TCUs, or Three Cam Units, open shallower cracks to active

cams. They are more likely to pivot out of cracks and rotate out of contact with the rock than four cam units. A runner cuts down on this tendency, as well as "walking" problems. Wired Bliss, the original TCUs, are shorter, lighter than other units, and very well made. The original models were a little awkward—you had to work the trigger bar from outside the cables. Wired Bliss can now be adjusted with one or two fingers inside the cable, so you are less likely to drop one. Metolius and Clog also make good units.

CMI ROKJOX are active single cable cams that work like active wedges. They are shallow, but the single cam could be tricky. They tried this same design as a passive cam many years ago; it worked but didn't catch on.

The rack

Arranging the tools of free climbing is a highly personal matter. Every climber is absolutely convinced of the superiority of his system. The only rule is this: if it works for you, it is the best.

The areas of agreement are few. Some climbers use two racks, one with quickdraws and free carabiners, the other with the chocks. The ancients always carried just one rack, on their left side (because the hammer was on the right). Only some experimentation will tell you which side is best for you. You may even change sides if a particular climb dictates this. A long, right-facing inside corner would be harder to do if you racked on the right, for example.

If you are going to swing leads with your partner, you have to reach some kind of agreement about what is going to be used. Swinging leads is the most efficient and speedy way for people of equal ability to get up a climb. It makes rope management easier and gives each climber a chance to rest without holding up progress. But you have to compromise on the racking.

You can rack gear on an ordinary runner, but 1-inch webbing is a little difficult to work with. Some climbers use $9/16$-inch supertape. That's fine if the rack is very light, but anything substantial would dig in before long. Chouinard, Dolt, and Clan Robertson make racking slings out of 2-inch webbing with the bottom rolled and sewn into 9mm size. When new, these slings can be used as part of the

The rack, with a mix of high-tech and Stone Age tools. The padded adjustable sling holds free carabiners, wired wedges, hexes, TCUs, Friends, and quickdraws. The half-length runners are girth-hitched to the sling: a tug on the outside loop frees the runner instantly. Another sling would carry more free carabiners and runners. While this rack might do for Eastern free climbing, it might be laughably weird for other applications.

belay, since they are plenty strong. Dolt makes a padded model, which is great for a heavy, big-wall rack. Chouinard and Forrest make 2-inch slings sewn to an 8mm rope racking section, neither of which is strong enough to be used as part of the belay. The Forrest is slightly padded; the Chouinard has a patch of Velcro hooks to grab clothing and minimize swinging of the rack.

All of these commercially produced slings come in a number of sizes. The idea is to get one that keeps the equipment close to your body without constricting movement. The correct size may vary with the amount of clothing you are wearing. Some people use a small sling over a T-shirt in the summer and a larger one over a sweater or pile jacket in cooler weather. Too long a sling leaves equipment banging around, often throwing you off balance, if not catching on something at the worst possible moment. When swinging leads, you may have to compromise — again. When I climb with someone over 6 feet tall, his large sling inevitably leaves chocks hanging down below my knees, but if he can struggle into a medium, I can live with a little extra length. Adjustable gear slings are available, and worth carrying if you are part of a Mutt & Jeff climbing partnership.

How are you going to arrange all the hardware? In general, free carabiners can be carried at the front, clipped with gates up and toward the body, in chains of two or three. Then come the chocks, from smaller to larger (the larger, heavier chocks will push the small ones forward). It is helpful to put wedges, especially those on wires, in front of hexes.

Some climbers rack each piece on its own carabiner; others find this too heavy and expensive. If you can look at a crack and pretty well judge which size nut you want, you can rack several chocks on a carabiner with the gate opening out and down (oval 'biners work best for racking multiple nuts). You then open the gate with your thumb and select the right chock with your fingers. If you can't tell by looking, rack several chocks of nearly the same size on one carabiner, gate opening up and in (in this case it doesn't matter much what type of carabiner you use). You then remove the carabiner from the rack, try several nuts until you find the right size, then remove the carabiner from that nut, and reattach it to the rack.

I rack large nuts individually because the large rope or webbing slings get too crowded if several are clipped into the same carabiner. I can never tell sizes of wedges, so I rack them in groups with the carabiner gates opening up and in.

So it's free carabiners first, small to larger wedges, then small to large hexes, followed by Friends. The number of each varies from area to area and climb to climb. Behind the nuts I carry several quickdraw runners (5 feet of 9/16-inch supertape clipped doubled between two carabiners), half-length runners (3 feet of 9/16-inch), and hero loops (2 feet of ½-inch) girth-hitched to the racking sling. Correctly tied, these slings can be tugged loose instantly, yet they stay secure and do not require the weight of extra carabiners.

There follows a sample rack for Eastern crag climbing. I include this because it is the most requested information among my students. Experienced climbers will inevitably criticize something because it isn't exactly the way they do it, but beginners find this suggestion helpful.

Rack sample for a beginner:
1. Free carabiners in chains of two or three
2. Carabiner, Chouinard wired stoppers #6 and #7
3. Carabiner, Chouinard wired hexes #1 and #2
4. Carabiner, Chouinard hexes #3 and #4 on Kevlar or Spectra
5. Hexes #5 through #8, each on about 4 feet of a different-color 8mm perlon, or 1-inch webbing, Kevlar or Spectra
6. Two to three 5-foot quickdraws of 9/16-inch, with some ridge-less ovals or offset Ds for fixed pins
7. 2-foot loops of ½-inch and 3-foot loops of 9/16-inch girth-hitched to the rack

Carried over the shoulder:
1. Larger hexes, on 6 feet of 1-inch webbing, or shorter loops of Kevlar or Spectra, if the climb requires them
2. One double runner (10 feet) of 1-inch webbing, either flat or cheap white tubular
3. 1-inch webbing runners, about 6 feet, each a different color

Folks climbing in the granite ranges of the West are more likely to want large Friends, Camalots, and Tri-Cams. Small Tri-Cams might substitute for the Eastern climber's wired hexes; they work well in pin scars. Parallel-sided granite cracks are cam territory.

You can often substitute 5.5mm Spectra cord or Kevlar for chock slings. The strong, thin cords are lighter and can make it easier to place the nuts. There has been some controversy about Kevlar, however. The Kevlar cord made by Yale Cordage and distributed by Chouinard is good for chock slings but nothing else.

Problems seem to arise when Kevlar takes too sharp a bend, so you might use Spectra cord for the smallest nuts. Kevlar has its limits, as I found out when handed a bulletproof vest of the stuff. "By the way, a good knife will cut through this like butter," I was told. Kevlar cord appears very resistant to cutting, but it is heavy, and you should avoid flexing and retying it. Manufacturer's tests on the polyethylene-based Spectra claim greater strength and abrasion resistance.

That's the minimum. Smaller stoppers, brass nuts, and Friends can be added. A rack of about a dozen nuts, a dozen runners, and 25 carabiners is a good place to start. Beginning climbers tend to use more nuts, more runners, and larger nuts, than climbers doing harder routes, who tend to want shorter runners and probably smaller nuts.

The bottom line is to carry what works for you and what you need to do a particular day's climb in safety with a feeling of security. With careful selection, the whole mess can be kept under 6 pounds — a far cry from the old piton racks.

Harnesses

The simplest way to attach oneself to the climbing rope is the bowline on a coil. But this takes up a good amount of rope, is not very comfortable to fall on, and just isn't convenient as part of a belay anchor.

Somewhat more convenient is a swami belt, 10 to 12 feet of 1-inch or 2-inch webbing wrapped around the waist and tied with a ring bend. This is not a lot more comfortable, or much safer in a fall, but it is quick, cheap, and effective. There are some commercial sewn swamis. For a lot of American climbers this is still the way to go. Simplicity is its greatest appeal. You can combine it with a runner for improvised leg loops.

Seat harnesses can be tied from webbing, but they tend to be more trouble than they are worth.

Sewn harnesses evolved from the swami and leg loop combinations. They are more comfortable, safer to fall in and make belaying and rappelling easier. If you want a harness, the criteria for selection should be fit, your style of climbing, and price.

All harnesses come in a range of sizes, but the dividing lines between sizes vary from manufacturer to manufacturer. The point of attachment of one harness may be better for you than another, because it is more likely to keep you upright in a fall. The only way to judge the fit and effectiveness of a harness is to try it on and compare it with other models. Hang in it for a while.

Various features can include gear loops, belay loops, hammer holster attachment points, adjustable leg loops, padding in the waist belt. It depends on what you want from a harness. If you use a belay device and attach it to the harness, select a harness with convenient attachment points for both the device and the belay anchor. A harness with secure points only at the front might be a poor choice. Using the harness as part of the belay chain makes setting up belays faster, more convenient, and safer because your body becomes a shock absorber.

You may want to choose an adjustable harness that can cover the range of clothing you might wear through all four seasons. Selecting a small harness to fit snug around your climbing shorts would be a big mistake if you intend to wear it over wool knickers and Goretex pants when you go ice climbing. By the same token, you might not notice the absence of hammer holster tabs in the summer, but you will wonder what to do with your alpine hammer come January.

There are three major harness manufacturers: Forrest, Troll, and Chouinard.

Forrest makes a two-piece harness, swami plus leg loops, that has been around for years and is a proven design. He also produces a one-piece seat harness in both a men's and a women's model, with a belay loop. All of his harnesses have provisions for equipment loops.

The classic Troll Whillans harness is still around. It is a good one-piece harness, though not as comfortable as the newer Mark VI and the lighter Freestyle. The Mark VI is a two-piece with sized or

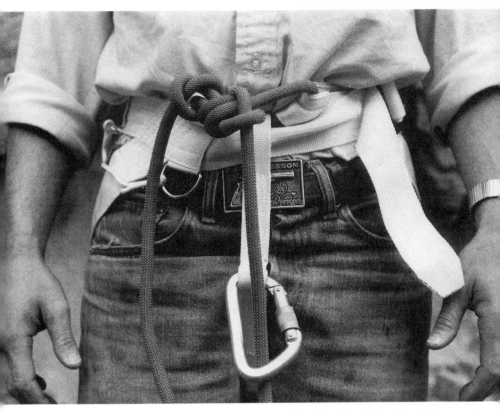

The venerable Whillans climbing harness with a bowline tie-in. The figure-eight is a more idiot-proof tie-in, but the bowline is a good knot to know, since it has other applications. If you don't use the bowline often enough, you tend to forget exactly how to tie it. Don't set up a situation that could force the carabiner into the buckle. Theoretically, the 'biner could make the buckle slip. (Note the S&W belt buckle — West Virginia chic.)

adjustable leg loops. The Freestyle is similar but the export model lacks equipment loops (the British model comes with them). The Freestyle does not need hammer holster tabs, since you can slide the holster over the waist belt. The Mark VI inexplicably has one tab on the left side. To put a hammer on the right, you would have to find a Troll or other holster with 3-inch slots. The Mark VI is the ultimate in comfort and convenience, with two bombproof belay loops and a padded waist. The Freestyle is the same design with thinner, lighter materials. Both offer a good fit and are quite comfortable during climbing.

The Chouinard harness is made to be used with a chest harness. Though it fits well and does not appear to have a tie-in point much lower than other seat harnesses, Chouinard does not advise use of the seat harness alone. The seat and chest combination, he says, will leave a climber supported at the ideal angle after a fall, and also minimize the chance of a head-first fall.

How a climber should be supported after a fall is a matter of some controversy. Europeans, who dominate the U.I.A.A., demand a vertical position and thus a full-body harness, if not a chest and seat combination; they are more concerned about how an unconscious climber would be supported than whether a harness works for climbing. The problem is that research on what the optimum position should be is conflicting and incomplete. The two studies done in the United States and Canada don't agree on the physiological effects of hanging in some of the existing harnesses. About the only area of agreement is that hanging in any harness, even a good one, is damned uncomfortable.

Chouinard's attempt at introducing an inexpensive, nonconstricting seat and chest combination may be a good idea in theory, but the practice is not catching on, and full-body harnesses may never achieve popularity on this side of the Atlantic. The narrow range of each size of the Chouinard harness necessitates buying several to cover climbing in all seasons. Some features of the Chouinard are very nice: the use of polyester webbing that won't weaken from exposure to sunlight, and contrasting color thread to make wear easier to spot.

Chest harnesses, compatible with seat harnesses, have been available for years from Troll, yet they are rarely seen in America. The number of falls successfully held by Forrest two-piece and Troll Whillans one-piece harnesses over the last ten years indicates that the seat harness works, to the satisfaction of American climbers. There are some situations where a chest harness is a nice addition, for example, glacier travel with a heavy pack. You can use a double runner (10 feet) in a figure-eight around the shoulders and clipped together in front. The climbing rope runs from the seat harness, through the carabiner at the front of the chest harness.

Chouinard's Bod Harness also comes in alpine and swami styles. It has very clean lines, and most people find it comfortable.

Todd Bibler made a great harness. It was very light and used a lower rear strap that pulled under the buttocks in a fall. There were no leg loops, so you could put it on while wearing crampons, skis, or snowshoes. Women found it very convenient. In a crowded marketplace, however, it never caught on.

Wild Country markets the Pat Littlejohn Harness, which uses several buckles to provide adjustability. It may be a one-size-fits-nobody harness. Wild Country's Gunfighter has lots of racking attachments, aimed at extreme climbers who are leading climbs with just quickdraws (often because the dogs have previewed the route or even preplaced protection). Quickdraws are all you need for clip and go.

The Gendarme's unique design for a one-piece swami employs a solid webbing with internal slots. No sizes, and only one sewn seam to attach the buckle. It is very popular with schools and clubs, since it is totally adjustable (not to mention comparatively cheap). Law enforcement agencies and closet commandos like the low-profile basic black and the nonrestrictive leg loops.

Padded swami belts (made by J Rat, Wild Things, Misty Mountain Threadworks, among others) offer the greatest comfort for rock climbing. Some use tubular webbing for a knotted closure; others use a buckle. Buckles used to dig into your ribs while you were catching a fall. Recent designs use smaller buckles, which are covered by the swami when you bend at the waist. Another advantage of the swami is that you can replace the matching leg loops, which wear out a lot faster than the waist section. You could top-rope with just the swami, then add the leg loops when lead climbing.

For rock climbing, I use a bunting-lined swami with leg loops. I found that 3-inch wide leg loops got in the way, but 2-inch worked fine. For ice climbing and mountaineering, I use a Gendarme Harness. It is very light and simple, it adjusts for extra clothes, and it allows tool holsters to slide on easily.

How long does a harness last? Troll figures three or four years of average use, and their experience is probably the broadest in the industry. You should inspect your harness regularly, looking for signs of wear on the parts that actually connect you to the rope. Any part of the harness that is used in rappel or belay should be carefully scrutinized. If you are getting nervous about committing to a rappel with your harness, retire it. You can rig a short runner through the tie-in points or around the waist belt to back up a suspect crotch loop or belay loop. Some Whillans models with 19mm crotch straps have broken in severe falls, according to *Mountain* magazine. Older models had a 25mm strap; none broke. Needless to say, if you are running a Sticht plate belay off one of these straps, you had better have a close look at it.

Using a harness as part of the belay system means that it is being subjected to at least some impact force. Just as with ropes and webbing, the energy-absorbing capacity of a harness is limited. No one has ever suggested retiring a harness after five falls, but perhaps it is time someone did.

One final caution about harnesses. As buckles on harnesses and swamis have gotten smaller, the carabiners used for belay and rappel devices have gotten bigger. Though it hasn't yet happened in the field, Chouinard's lab tests have shown that a large carabiner can lever the buckle open. This could conceivably happen if you were anchored from behind or the right side, say, and were pulled leftward by a fall, toward the buckle. The easiest way to minimize this risk is to tie the climbing rope in between the buckle and any central carabiner. The rope is then much less likely to be able to force the buckle to slide.

Shoes

Climbers may be secret foot fetishists; there is more talk about shoes than any other item of equipment. Various shoes have been endowed with magical properties. "If only I had better shoes, I could lead 5.10" is a common lament. It is true that a beginner will notice a big difference climbing with good shoes. They make getting started in the sport a lot less painful. Some shoes are better than others, but the best shoe for you is the one that fits best and is suited for your kind of climbing.

Climbing started in sneakers and nailed boots. A lot of climbers still do easy routes in sneakers. The more exotic running shoes are less useful than their simpler predecessors because they have flared heels, thick, soft midsoles and patterned soles — all to absorb the impact of running. A simple training shoe can sometimes fill the bill.

If you have been climbing since God was a little boy, you may remember the early kletterschuhe. This was a lightweight, split-grain leather boot with a rubber Vibram-like sole. It was flexible enough for hiking and some rudimentary friction climbing. Such light hiking boots are now making a comeback with high-tech Gore-tex uppers. The kletterschuhe never disappeared, actually. Kastinger still makes the Kletter, and Fabiano, the Madre. They haven't changed much in twenty years and they still work quite well for moderate rock climbing. There is a lot to be said for a boot that can be used for an approach, even days of backpacking, and then used on the climb.

A similar boot was produced by the French company Galibier. Originally called the RR and later the Yosemite, these blue suede shoes were the ultimate climbing shoe for a long time. If you can get a good price on a used pair, buy them. If you have an old pair in the closet, try getting them resoled with an Ascender sole or Vibram's newest soft climbing lug sole. Careful craftsmanship in the resoling can improve their performance, and you will climb better than you did with their original, hard Galibier sole.

Today, all climbing shoes are *varappes,* or friction shoes. They have smooth rubber soles for maximum contact and adhesion to the rock. Galibier dominated the market for almost thirty years, until others introduced stickier rubber soles.

The first sticky-sole shoe was the Fire, made in Spain by Boreal.

The rubber was soon copied and became the standard. An American company, 5.10, developed a longer-wearing sticky formula; it became the rubber of choice for resoling.

Fires are still around. The original model has been redesigned several times for an improved fit. It is still an all-leather shoe and stretches as much as two full sizes with use. The Fire Cat is canvas-lined to minimize stretching and increase lateral stability. There is a Big Wall model to fill the gap left by the scarcity of traditional edging shoes. A Ballet for limestone and a slipper called Ninja were added to the line, along with a low-cut model. (Change is a constant in shoe design.) Another Spanish company, Calma, makes similar shoes. They offer an inexpensive start in climbing shoes, especially for wide feet.

Don't overlook slippers as a cheap starter. These ballet shoes don't last long, but they are great to carry on alpine climbs, and on many extreme climbs, they offer real advantages. Their thin soles give the ultimate in friction and are more comfortable than a regular shoe on friction climbs. You can also get your feet into tiny cracks; it's a real surprise to find yourself walking a 5.10 finger crack. I thought toe jams would be painful, but the leather uppers, not my feet, take the beating. The elastic at the heel may dig in after a while, especially if you walk in them, so take them off at belays and tape your heels.

Galibier has the E.B. Passion, a stiff, wide, nylon shoe, a favorite at Smith Rock. Galibier sells an inexpensive boot and a very expensive edging shoe with a removable insole. Resin Rose shoes are made by a French company, One Sport, and have a thin metal shank. Newer models use a carbon fiber shank and carry a stupefying price. Kamet makes the Joshua Tree and Fantasy, both lined with Cambrelle, to minimize stretching.

A milestone in shoe design was the work of Heinz Mariacher for La Sportiva. An instep strap and higher heel banding give improved snugness and control. Front lacing holes are closely spaced, with a hinge-like notch above the instep. Upper lace holes have metal eyelets, so you can crank down on the laces. Mariacher design principles are used in the Merrell Smear, Asolo On Sight, Scarpa Spider, and 5.10 Vertical. They function the same way, so pick the best fit.

Sportiva makes a unifoot design. At each wearing the climber is supposed to switch the shoe from one foot to the other to distribute wear on both sides. Cute idea, but you always feel awkward, like your shoes don't fit.

Today's hot shoes are derived from designs for limestone climbing in Europe. They are stiff, so you can edge with the toe straight into small pockets in the rock, often on overhanging rock, where it is easier on the arms if you are on your toes. The shoes are cut low, supposedly allowing higher steps in face climbing. The ankle coverage, useful in crack climbing, is thus sacrificed. A few years ago, the extreme flexibility of the Fire was most sought after. Now it's the stiff Eurodog shoes, even though they may be too specialized for most climbing. Again, don't buy a shoe because some famous climber uses them — buy the shoe that will suit you.

The first criterion in selecting any climbing shoe is the fit. That pretty much determines which shoe you will use, at least among friction shoes. The idea is to have your toe right up to the end of the shoe. As long as your toes are not pushed back so that they are arched and cannot lie flat, the shoes are not too small. With a light sock, they should feel snug. If one toe is being squeezed on top of another, try a wider shoe. There should be just enough room for your toes — you will only slide around in any additional room.

Try the shoes on and leave them on for a while. Don't believe anybody who says they have to be excruciating to climb right. All of these shoes are handmade, so try several pairs of the same size. One pair may fit noticeably better than the others. The main difference in shoes is width, but uppers now wrap around the foot, the better to fit a variety of widths. If you have any foot problems, think about where each shoe might give you trouble. A lot of designs use an instep strap, which can be uncomfortable if you have a high arch.

Thin wool socks like Wigwam's Summit seem to work best. They don't wrinkle and last pretty well. I checked with marathon runners to see if something else might last longer, but they were using the same sock for their training. Polypropylene liner socks work well but don't give the feet much padding. You'll have sore feet anyway early in the season, but climbing toughens them up.

The price of shoes now mandates resoling. Since you end up resoling with 5.10 rubber, differences in rubber aren't as important as they used to be. For somebody to do the work, try Steve Komito of Estes Park, Colorado, or Wheeler & Wilson of Bishop, California.

There is no excuse for the climbing prices of climbing shoes: not inflation, not materials, not exchange rates. It must be naked greed. When ropes reached $150, the market crashed, new producers entered, and prices were miraculously cut in half. Let's hope the same thing happens with shoes. In any case, an American-made climbing shoe is long overdue.

Helmets

Most American climbers do not wear helmets; elsewhere in the world, the use of helmets is more common. Whether you must have one depends on where you climb. In an area with good granite, like Yosemite, there are few loose rocks. People are pretty well spread out, too, so you're less likely to get clobbered by climber-generated rockfall. A helmet makes more sense at Seneca, where there is always something coming down. Though it is true that a helmet can also protect your head in a fall, helmets are just too uncomfortable to wear for that reason alone. Basically, you wear one out of fear of rockfall.

Helmets are a nuisance: they are uncomfortable, expensive, hard to fit in a pack, awkward to carry around, and heavy—a general pain in the ass. Worst of all, they are an admission that something nasty could happen to you. Most climbers believe they lead charmed lives. "I'm good," they reason, "and you don't get rockfall on hard climbs." They see the helmet as the badge of the eternal 5.4 climber.

A British friend noted that I was the only American he knew who always wore a helmet when climbing. It was ironic, then, that I would get a fractured skull while standing protected by an overhang watching a friend do a 5.10. A hold pulled off and smashed into a ledge above us. One piece went up into an inside corner, then bounced straight at me. It was about as improbable as getting hit by a piece of Skylab. I wasn't wearing my helmet because I wasn't climbing. I hit the ground with my lights out, and only the efforts of my friends saved my life and prevented any brain damage.

As I lay in the hospital awaiting the results of a brain scan, I wasn't frightened, but I was deeply saddened by the idea that something I loved as much as climbing could leave me impaired for life. I was lucky. I was left with just a trace of a scar.

Had that been my only close call, I might dismiss it, but it was my second; my third followed several months later. Rockfall is a fact of life in some areas—it comes with the territory. I still curse my helmet, but I always wear it.

If you feel you need one, get one that you will wear. Buy a light-colored one so that it won't be any hotter than it has to be. Get the right size. The shell of most helmets should cover the top of your ears and part of your forehead. If it is too big, it will be slipping down into your field of vision and covering your ears and affecting your balance. If it is too small, it is worthless. Very critical parts of your brain are at the lower rear and upper front areas of your skull—you know, the frontal lobes, the stuff you are reading this book with.

There are a number of helmets available in the United States: Joe Brown (JB), Mountain Safety Research (MSR), Ultimate, and several models produced by Romer.

An adjustable helmet, like the JB or Ultimate, is good because it allows you to add a balaclava or watch cap in winter. Most ice climbers wear helmets because there are all those pieces of ice flying around. The MSR is sized to fit your head with foam tape, which makes a great fit, but it also makes it hard to get a balaclava inside.

In warm weather the MSR is most comfortable because it is both very light and vented. (No, it doesn't rain in the vent holes and I don't know why.) A JB lightweight is much more comfortable than the super, especially if it is a light color (white or yellow).

The Face Nord, a light, vented helmet, offers great comfort and price and only marginally less protection. Wild Country makes a similar helmet, as does Petzl. All of these helmets meet the U.I.A.A. standards for top impact, frontal impact, top penetration, and chin strap stretch. But even nonclimbing helmets designed for canoeing, biking, or construction may be better than nothing in an area known for loose rock.

You're still not convinced that you should wear protection? Of course, the contents of some climbers' heads are not worth the price of a helmet.

Belaying and rappelling devices

Today the limits of free climbing are being explored—and pushed—by people who are willing to fall. Technology is making that willingness something less than suicidal. If all of those falls were caught with body belays, you would have to use a gun to recruit your belayers.

The device that has withstood the test of time is the Sticht plate. It is usually seen in this country with one 11mm slot and one 9mm, although they come in double 11mm and double 9mm. The double 11mm can be used to rappel, but it is hard on the rope, and the double 9mm is not necessary since the 9–11mm works just as well on two 9mm ropes. You can get them with a spring, which is supposed to help keep the plate from jamming during normal use. The spring works, sort of, but it is always catching on things while you're climbing. Once you get used to a plate without one, that works just as well.

Forrest is now selling the PBI plate, which looks like the original Sticht plates: rectangular with one 11mm slot. The PBI is smaller, thinner and lighter. The edges of the slots are square and would be a little rough on the rope if you are sloppy about feeding it through. It is priced a few dollars less than the Sticht.

The plates come drilled with a couple of holes for a small retaining cord. To use the plate, you feed a bight (loop) of the rope through the slot and clip it into a carabiner. During a fall, the impact force and the pull of the brake hand jam the rope between plate and carabiner. This sounds pretty tough on the rope, but it does it no harm. The retaining cord keeps the plate within a few inches of the 'biner. A U-shaped cord, stiffened by a wrapping of athletic tape, will work much like the spring—without the added cost, weight, and hassle.

This device is not an automatic belay, nor is it entirely static. You have to exert some pressure to lock the plate. The second, belaying the leader, has gravity working for him, but a leader belaying a second from above has to be more careful about pulling the rope to lock the plate. Pull your hand down, not just parallel with the plate. If you hold the rope parallel, some of it will feed through in a hard fall. Even a second falling without much slack can pull some rope through unless you pull down sharply with the brake hand.

There have been some lawsuits in Europe because people thought the plate worked automatically. In some cases, with sloppy belay anchors, the belayers were pulled upside down and lost the advantage of gravity; they were too surprised, too weak, or too ignorant to pull the plate tight. Many European climbing books refer to the plate as a dynamic belaying device, and this is true. In a severe fall, rope will start to run through the plate. Only a short distance of rope (rarely more than one foot) is needed to make the belay dynamic enough to stop any fall. The force at which the belay becomes dynamic is much higher than it would be in a body belay. Though the plate is dynamic, it is less dynamic than a body belay. If you want a more dynamic belay, simply hold the brake hand parallel to the plate for a moment before pulling down. That will allow a foot or so of rope to be pulled through by a hard fall—just enough rope to decrease impact forces greatly.

The plate does not do the job for you. You have to use both hands to maintain a smooth feed of the rope. If you get lazy, the thing will jam, spring or no spring. To minimize the risk of a jam, attach plate and rope to two carabiners, side by side.

Carefully inspect the inside of the slots of any plate for irregularities that would abrade the rope. Most plates require a touch-up with a file and emery paper.

You might buy a plate if you are doing double roping. There are several brands of superlight plates for double- or single-rope belays. Don't use them for top roping or rappelling, however, as there isn't enough metal to allow for much wear. The DMM Betterbrake is a full-sized double-slot plate with a concave surface to allow for much easier rope handling. The Clog Cosmic Arrester is similar. Forrest makes a second belay–rappel device called a Triton. Latok makes its Tuber in two sizes, for 9mm and 11mm ropes. For single 11mm rope the small hole of a figure 8 descender works almost as well, weighs a little more, but gives you two good tools for the price of one.

The figure 8 is just about idiot-proof as a descender. When used with a screwgate or two standard carabiners, it has never been known to fail. You simply slide a bight of rope through the large hole and over the shaft, then clip in. You can set it up for either hand to act as a brake. The only thing that can go wrong is allowing the rope to creep back up the shaft and form a girth hitch around the large ring. Fast descents or awkward beginners can provoke this situation. Russ Anderson makes several models with "ears" to prevent this. He also puts an 11mm belay slot in the center of the shaft. This would be a little easier to handle than using the small hole at one end.

The SMC straight 8 uses a more squared-off shape for added friction, and the small slot is D-shaped for easier use as a belay plate. It is a little harder to lock off on rappel, because of the squared edges of the large ring.

Clog, Colorado Mountain Industries (CMI), and Chouinard make simple, inexpensive, classic figure 8 descenders. Clog also makes a larger ring for rescue work and caving. The small holes are large enough for two carabiners and can be used for belay with an 11mm rope, though it sometimes takes a bit of persuasion to feed a stiff, old rope into the ring.

Two carabiners: remember that. You should use two standard 'biners to clip into the figure 8. The death of Tom Patey, who was starting a rappel off a sea stack in Scotland, was one of those instances when unpredictable forces force open the gate of a carabiner. Use two, with gates reversed and opposed.

One other caution: any figure 8 that is dropped — and many people do drop them while trying to feed in the rope — should be discarded. Most are drop-forged, and impact could cause hairline stress fractures. Since you are totally committed to the device while on rappel, any chance of a crack is unacceptable.

Most figure 8s have an anodized coating to protect the rope from the friction of a rappel. This may wear off with use, but CMI's coating is more likely to chip from banging around while the device is clipped to the harness. If it does chip, sand the edges of the damaged area to minimize the cutting of rope fibers this could cause. I had a nasty nick in mine from descending a scree slope and only noticed it the next time I went to rappel. It actually had a very sharp burr sticking out. A rough rock served in place of a file, and I could grind it down on the spot. Check your figure 8 periodically for irregularities.

One of the great advantages of the figure 8 is that you can lock off the device. This can make starting an awkward rappel much safer, and can allow you to stop in midrappel to free the ropes or to shoot some pictures.

Smaller figure 8s may not work on 11mm ropes. The Chouinard figure 8, with its slightly bent shaft to minimize twisting, is a prime example of a tool for 9mm ropes only; you really can't rappel with it on double 11mm ropes.

When using the 8 for belay with the small end, don't forget to rig some kind of retaining cord if the 8 is at all likely to get away from you. Some people belay using the same configuration as for rappel. Others regard this as unsafe, arguing that the brake hand could be pulled into the large ring, crushing fingers and causing the loss of the belay.

The Seilbremse was introduced from Switzerland by Yvon Chouinard. It is a forged alloy steel oval. Clipped to the harness, it supports a carabiner or two as rappel break bars. For belay, a bight of rope is passed through the oval and clipped to the harness, something like the figure 8. The technique looks very much like the rather suspect method of using the figure 8. The Seilbremse is smaller, so perhaps there is less likelihood that your hand will be pulled into it. Chouinard says this device gives a belay 13 percent greater stopping distance than the average of other techniques — that is, it offers a more dynamic belay and dramatically decreases the impact force of a fall. Tiny nuts, ice screws, and marginal snow anchors are less likely to rip out. There will be a slight increase in the distance of the fall, however, so think about spacing the runners more closely.

Some people have had real problems rappelling with the Seilbremse. A small piece of steel, it dissipates heat poorly. When several people have already rappelled down, the rope has been heated up and has some twists. The Seilbremse can get hot enough to burn you, or the rope. If you rappel quickly onto a twist in the rope, it will stop dead, and unlike the figure 8, it offers no easy, secure lock-off.

The Seilbremse is small and light, and therein lie both its chief advantage and its chief disadvantage. It is very easy to feed out rope, even two 9mm ropes, during belay. Since it is small and steel, there is less banging around while climbing, and it would be very difficult to damage it.

I have used the Seilbremse while teaching and found it to be a very useful and versatile tool. It need never be disconnected from the harness, since neither belay nor rappel requires it to be unclipped, and it is small and light enough not to be in the way while climbing. It does require a screwgate carabiner, since it is so small that it doesn't have room for two carabiners to clip in. You can jam the device by letting it slip onto the side of the carabiner; this is most likely when using old, fuzzy 9mm ropes. The cure is to pop the Seilbremse back onto the end of the carabiner and give the ropes a tug through it. With really cranky 9s, use some other device.

Using a Seilbremse, I have had no difficulty belaying students who were following me up climbs. Their falls did not pull any rope through the device, and there was no danger of getting my fingers pulled into it. The device makes it easy to take in rope quickly, so I could keep up with students moving up easy sections of climbs.

When you're rappelling, a figure 8 puts a twist in the rope. Knowing this, climbers don't untwist the ropes before they start the figure 8 will pass through any twists. This is a little rough rope but it doesn't stop the rappel.

ie Seilbremse, on the other hand, does not twist the rope — an advantage, since you are not perpetuating kinks by forcing them through. The rope is left unkinked and ready to pull down. The Seilbremse also works more evenly and slowly than the figure 8. A slower rappel does not work up as much heat and thus is better for the rope.

If I were a beginner, I would be tempted to buy this device instead of a figure 8. It doesn't cost much more, and you'll lose less time than you will fussing with plates or figure 8s, threading them for belay or rappel. The Seilbremse is quick to rig for either use, and it is always attached and ready.

Many people have tried the Munter hitch for belaying. It works and it is safe . . . sort of. To catch a fall, the knot has to reverse itself inside your carabiner. New carabiners made just for such use lessen the chance that the knot will jam, but the chance still exists. The possibility that the Munter hitch will jam on you just when you don't need anything more going on, or anything else to worry about, can give you pause. In my experience it doesn't work as smoothly as any of the devices and can be a real pain if the leader is yo-yoing, climbing up and down difficult moves to work them out or place protection. The Munter is not very convenient for belaying the second, either, as it doesn't move very fast and a kinky rope can turn it into a nightmare. I taught myself this knot when I started guiding: clients would drop their equipment, I would lend them mine (I figured that was safer than to count on their body belay), and since now I had no gear, I would use the Munter hitch. I soon stopped using it, though — it was more hassle than it was worth.

Having all the latest climbing equipment can provide some advantages, mental if nothing else, but it would be well to remember that despite all the new gizmos, climbing hasn't changed all that much. The process is the same as ever, and the high-tech tools are merely refinements. We aren't all that far from the climbers who filled their pockets with stones selected from a streambed.

8

TRAINING

The tradition of training with 12-ounce curls in a pub dies hard—some nights, harder than others. Climbers may be the last athletes to discover the benefits of an exercise program designed to improve their ability in their chosen activity. But it's true: if performance is important, training is important.

Maybe you don't have the time or desire to train hard for climbing; that's fine. Lots of people do recreational climbing, up to about 5.9, without any training. To climb harder, or to climb several times a week, training helps. But even very limited training can help the novice or intermediate become comfortable as a weekend climber. Just squeezing a ball with your hands and doing toe stands, for example, will develop the small muscles that are most used in climbing. You get maximum return for the time spent. Suddenly moves are less of a struggle, and the whole sport becomes more enjoyable.

A training program can be enormously complicated, but the results should be simple: you climb better. The problem is, there is not a lot of consensus here. In fact, on some matters the authorities give completely contradictory advice. Let's first look at some ways of improving your body's general condition and then get to the most efficient methods of improving climbing performance.

General conditioning

Cardiovascular endurance. You'll notice improvements in your cardiovascular system when you're lugging a pack full of ropes and hardware to the climbing site. CV workouts promote general good health, which is highly recommended for everybody, climbers included.

The CV workout is simple: 20 minutes three times a week at or above the training threshold. Training threshold?

$$(220 - \text{age}) \times 0.7 + \text{resting heart rate}$$

Or go by the Karvonen method:

$$(220 - \text{resting heart rate}) \times 0.7 + \text{resting heart rate}$$

Take your resting heart rate first thing in the morning, before you get out of bed.

For a CV workout, any exercise will do. Swimming, biking, and rowing are the most injury-free, but running is cheap and easy.

Besides strengthening your heart, CV workouts can burn blubber and lower your percentage of body fat. Extra pounds of fat are not always bad. For long climbs in extreme cold, in fact, carrying a few percentage points of fat above your normal level is good. Body fat is lighter to carry than food, and you can use it as energy without having to eat a thing. Altitude tends to kill your appetite, and cooking is a long, slow process in rarefied air, so having a few calories to spare can't hurt. Besides, it's insulation.

For hard rock, however, you don't need it. Elite male athletes have 5 percent to 12 percent body fat, and female athletes, 10 percent to 17 percent. Shedding body fat vastly increases your ratio of strength to body weight. Since body weight is what you're trying to move up the face of the rock, a lighter body can translate into the greatest degree of improvement for most recreational climbers. You want to go from 5.9 to 5.10? Lose a few pounds.

Diet. Whether you want to lose weight or just eat healthfully, avoid fats. Compare three diets: your more or less typical American menu (fast food, ice cream, and potato chips), a better diet (the kind recommended by most doctors for most people), and the Pritikin diet (eaten by those who are deeply into carbohydrate loading).

diet	carbohydrate	fat	protein
typical American	40%	25–30%	20–30%
better	60	15	25
Pritikin	80	5–10	10–15

Fat does provide the required fatty acids, fat-soluble vitamins, a lot of the taste of many foods, and the feeling of a full stomach. But fats contain about 9 calories per gram; protein and carbs yield only 4 calories (alcohol, by the way, gives you 7 calories per gram). The idea is to get the fuel you need without building up excess *body* fat.

Specialists have worked out good guidelines on nutrition for athletes. I use *The Athlete's Kitchen,* by Nancy Clark. Find something you can live with. It's also a good idea to know your own medical history, like your cholesterol count, and to take an honest look at the family records to see what might lie ahead.

Flexibility. Contrary to popular belief, you can hurt yourself by increasing flexibility. If you increase the range of motion of a joint without developing strength through the full range — especially through the new range of motion — you are asking for trouble. You have to have the strength to safely and effectively use the joint. Shoulders and knees are the prime offenders, but hip and leg flexibility are more important in climbing. Hip flexibility allows you to keep the hips closer to the rock, thus putting less weight on the hands. Flexible hamstrings and calf muscles will allow you to step higher.

Bob Anderson's *Stretching* is the best guide, even though he doesn't offer suggestions specifically for climbers. Select a few of his basic stretches for the legs, hips, and groin.

Another method is the PNF stretch. Spelling out the abbreviation would be deeply confusing. Let's just say it involves contraction after each stretch. You do an isometric contraction, then stretch farther than the last time. Repeat three times, for a total of four repetitions.

For climbers, one of the best PNF stretches would be the forward split. Stand with legs apart. Lean forward, hands to the mat, and work your legs straight out to the sides while lowering the forward part of your hips to the mat. The contraction is just coming back up. Repeat three times, stretching closer to the mat each time.

Coordination and agility. Coordination is getting the muscle groups to work together with balance to perform a desired action; agility is performing the action quickly and efficiently. No gym needed here. Just go bouldering. It develops both coordination and agility, along with strength and the ability to visualize moves in a sequence. It's a quick, highly specific, total workout — no equipment, no one else involved.

Strength and endurance. Strength is one maximal contraction of a muscle; endurance is multiple submaximal contractions. Strength training carries over into endurance — raising maximal contraction means you can do more submaximal contractions — much more than endurance training improves strength.

Training for strength involves recruiting muscle fibers to perform an action and building coordination of motor units (nerve cells and muscle fibers). By training just for endurance, you may not be stimulating all the fibers enough to develop such coordination as well. So if your training is limited by time (or by fear of injury or overtraining), concentrate on building strength.

The mix of strength versus endurance can vary muscle by muscle. Fingers might need more endurance work to increase the time you can hang on to small holds, for example, while the large muscles of the back and shoulders need strength training to help you make a move and recover quickly.

Training increases the muscles' capacity for work by increasing their fuel supply, capacity to eliminate the waste products of metabolism, and ability to refuel and recover for another contraction.

General principles

You probably spend more time chalking up, tying knots, and scoping out the route than actually climbing. It's an episodic sport. So do interval training. If you're doing pullups, for example, do only a few repetitions. Up to six reps is best for strength; beyond that you are working on endurance. You can use a weight to keep the intensity of pullups high and the reps down, but add weight only after you have worked up to it. Don't strap 50 pounds to yourself right away and expect not to do real damage to your shoulders.

Rest is important. The fuel for muscular contraction, ATP, regenerates 50 percent after 20 seconds and reaches 100 percent after 3 minutes, at which point the muscles have a full charge for the next contraction. Your muscles also need time to get rid of a waste product of ATP consumption, lactic acid. When your limbs begin to shake in the middle of a strenuous move, it's because lactic acid has built up in the muscle tissues from the burning of fuel without oxygen. At rest, the muscle starts to clear out this waste product and will have processed 100 percent in 75 minutes.

The best training exercises for climbing would correspond to these principles:

Specificity. The exercises are as much like climbing as possible.

Adaptation. The body adapts to increasing stress.

Intensity. High intensity, meaning heavy loads and low repetitions, works best.

Duration. The exercise period is short for strength, long for endurance.

Exercises

For the beginner, the muscles of the hands and feet are the weakest link. Every climber trying to get in shape, whether he's coming back from a winter layoff, an injury, or an attack of adulthood, has the same problem. The cure is surprisingly simple: climb. The best training for climbing really is climbing, but there are a couple of things you can do on rainy days to speed the training process. Rising up on your toes, then gently lowering, will quickly strengthen the foot and calf muscles. You may need to combine this

Rubber tubing or a bungi cord for the one-arm pullup. The cord takes some weight, assists in balance, and helps prevent injury when you lower.

Another one-arm pullup, raising the stack of weights on a Universal. John has a hundred-pound weight in his lap to keep himself on the floor.

To increase the intensity of a pullup workout, attach extra weight to a belt and tell yourself it's a big-wall rack.

with exercises to stretch the Achilles tendon, to keep flexibility. Squeezing a rubber ball with 70 percent of your strength will develop your forearms and hands. Spring grips and rubber donuts develop only the forearm; squeezing the ball and holding the contraction do a better job of mimicking the action of climbing.

The pulling muscles of the biceps and back are most important for climbers. But you should also develop some pushing muscles, the triceps and chest, for offwidth cracks, mantles, counterpressure, and chimneys.

When you go to work out, try to mimic the climbing motion. If you're using a lat machine, put the bar in front of you, not behind (as most nonclimbing trainers would have you do): the rock face is in front of you, right? Likewise, all hand and finger exercises should be isometric. The rock doesn't move, so you shouldn't move your fingers during finger exercises. The common spring hand grips may simulate hand action for crack climbing, but they are not very good for developing strength for hanging on to holds.

Isometric contraction builds strength at only one point in the range of motion—only the angle you are training at. To build strength over the whole range, you must vary the angle of the joint. For example, when you're doing pullups, lock off at various points. About chest height is where you will lock off most during climbing, since if you go any higher, your center of gravity will shift outward, making it more difficult to hold on. The training would still be beneficial but less specific for most climbing.

To mimic climbing using a bar, don't put your thumb underneath. Not many handholds offer a place where you can curl your thumb inside to help pull you up.

Start any workout with exercises for larger body parts, then get down to the smaller ones. For example:

1. Warmups: short cardiovascular workout, stretching, simple calisthenics.

2. Pullups: for back and shoulders.

3. Dips: for chest muscles.

4. Rowing: for lats (back) and biceps (bend over and use a barbell).

5. Rope climbing: for back, shoulders, and arms (hand over hand).

6. Front lever or iron cross: for back and shoulders.

7. Curls: for biceps.

8. Reverse curls: to prevent injury to the biceps (more about this shortly).

9. Preacher curls: for biceps (kneel or sit and use a bench).

There are several devices that work especially well for climbers. The finger board will remind you of pullups on a door frame. It can be a board about 3 feet wide by 2 inches deep, with variously shaped pieces of wood, each ½ inch deep, nailed to it at various angles. You can loosen up on the board itself, then switch to the holds and move from hold to hold just as if you were climbing. Vary the workout: a wide grip works the shoulder muscles, a narrow grip concentrates on the arm muscles. Lock off on one hand by keeping the wrist straight up and down, the elbow flexed at about a right angle; move the shoulder to get your center of gravity under your hand.

For the affluent there are now climbing simulators, with a whole variety of excruciating holds. These are constructed from epoxy mixed with sand, which gives a good grip and toughens the hands. For a lot of people, they make a real difference in climbing ability.

People used to just climb a rope, hand over hand, to develop their grip and upper body. It still works, and it's a lot cheaper than a simulator, but it's not as jazzy. The truly devoted used to construct wooden crack machines to practice jams. Making such a crack gave them more of a workout than actually using it: they had to sand the wood endlessly to avoid terminal splinters.

Preventing injuries

The most common climbing injury is not broken bones from leader falls but tendinitis from death grips on tiny face holds. Your own strength can damage tissues.

To keep strength evenly balanced on both sides of a joint, train antagonistic muscles. Have a 2:1 or 3:1 ratio for such strength. If

The preacher curl. The bench lessens the risk of elbow injury and gives you a different range of motion than a regular curl.

A homemade but very effective simulator. It has angled, round, and horizontal holds of various sizes, and several types of pockets. The pieces are attached with countersunk wood screws. Lots of sanding was needed, but that's great for climber's fingers.

The basic lock-off at shoulder height. But he'd better watch the ceiling — or don a helmet.

you can do nine pullups, for example, you should be able to do three dips. For the inverse of wrist flexion, the basic wrist motion of climbing, work on reverse wrist curls. For fingers, the old trick is to put a rubber band around the thumb and one finger at a time. Pull them apart. Medical supply stores sell a rubber ring attached to a small ball so that you can accomplish the same thing without snapping lots of rubber bands.

The lower back is a prime site of trouble for climbers. You need to do regular exercises to stretch the lower back muscles and strengthen the abdominals. Here's the simplest: lie on your back, knees up. Bring your knees to your chest, hold them in with your hands, count to 10 and release, then repeat.

If you're working out, you may find very quickly that you have to cut back the exercises to avoid injury. Especially if you are climbing regularly, you don't want to overdo the exercises. The most notorious device for self-destruction is the Bachar ladder. Lengths of 2-inch PVC pipe are covered with tape, drilled and tied together with an old climbing rope, then suspended to hang free. The climber does laps, swinging from rung to rung. He is guaranteed to develop massive lats and sore elbows.

To exercise the muscles antagonistic to those worked on the

Bachar ladder, in a way that's a lot less stressful on the elbows, you can use parallel bars. Get up on the bars and lower yourself slowly, so that your waist is well below the bars, then raise yourself back up, slowly. It's good for the shoulders.

Workout cycle

You can't do the same workout every day and have it do any good. You need to change both content and order. As part of a cycle leading to a peak, you drop repetitions and increase intensity while perfecting your technique.

You might, for example, start out in the dead of winter in the weight room with light weights. Increase the weight and drop the reps to build strength. As the climbing season starts in the spring, you cut weight training back to twice a week and spend more time on the specific activity, climbing, while using the weights to maintain your level of strength.

How hard should a workout be? If 100 percent is total exhaustion, anything over 90 percent is a heavy workout, 70 percent to 90 percent is medium, and anything below 70 percent is light.

Light workouts should always follow heavy workouts. A weekend climber could rest on Monday, do a heavy workout on Tuesday, work on technique Wednesday, then go for another heavy workout on Thursday. Friday might be a light workout or travel to the weekend's climb. The training principle here is stress–recover–stress–recover.

How do you know how much to do? Start out easy, and use common sense. Training may be painful, but the pain of simple muscle soreness should go away within 24 hours. When you start training, your performance may actually drop for the first two to three weeks. Be patient. But later on, a drop in performance can be a sign of overtraining. First tinker with the formula by changing repetitions and weights. If you don't see an improvement, do less. Stop if you have to.

Besides persistent muscle soreness, the signs of overtraining are insomnia, irritability, swollen lymph glands, loss of weight or appetite. If you suspect you've overdone it, check your resting heart rate first thing in the morning. A jump of over six beats per minute indicates you are probably overtraining. That's not exactly scientific, but athletes all over the world are trying to come up with a more precise measure, and Siberia is populated with coaches who didn't get it right.

Training, after all, is stressing your body. Most of the time it is a healthy experience, even serving as an outlet for emotional stress. But sometimes it just doesn't work that way, and other aspects of your life sneak into your physical performance. You can train and exercise successfully for years, then something throws you off. While I was writing this chapter and working on the illustrations for this book, my performance dropped for the first time in ten years, and I had all the symptoms of overtraining.

CLIMBING INSTRUCTION

At some point, every climber has to evaluate a prospective partner. In addition, more people are seeking professional instruction. What is the minimum amount of knowledge any climber must possess? To find out, let's take a look at a typical course.

First, the instructor issues equipment. (If only top roping is to be done, there is nothing to issue.) A harness, a helmet, carabiners, a descender, a runner, and a Prusik sling are necessary for any course dealing with pitch climbing and descent. After the instructor issues the equipment, he shows the students how to use each item (except the descender, which the students learn to use later).

Once the equipment is collected, the group troops off to an appropriate site. The best site for beginners is a short cliff with an easy path up and a broad summit. The instructor now demonstrates the basic tie-in knot. My preference is the figure-eight, or Flemish bend. It is the strongest known, it is almost foolproof, and variations on it can be used for anchors. Each student must be able to tie the figure-eight knot into his harness and add a half-double fisherman's knot as a stopper knot. This is also a good time for the instructor to demonstrate the figure-eight loop and for the students to master it.

The instructor now rigs two anchors, one near the edge of the cliff and the other a few feet back. The first anchor, with two carabiners, can be used for the rappel line and later as a top-rope climbing rig. The second anchor is for a belayer, since all students should be belayed with a second rope on their first rappels. When constructing these anchors, the instructor can demonstrate the bowline and review the figure-eight loop. He can also show how to tie into the back of the harness with a figure-eight loop, creating a belay without any hardware.

Now the students learn how to take in and feed out rope, and to conduct a proper belay. They must master the body belay before using the Sticht plate or similar device. When they all have had a go at it and seem comfortable, the instructor can demonstrate a rappel, using a figure 8 descender and a Prusik safety. Each student rappels in turn while being belayed by another student.

At this point, the students have learned belaying, rappelling, and all the basic knots. They learn the body rappel for the same reason the body belay is taught: they must be able to perform vital actions without relying on equipment. Next they construct a carabiner brake assembly, and use this to rappel.

There remains one crucial lesson: how to tie off a fallen leader. Under no circumstances should anyone climb with someone who has not mastered this procedure. If body belays are used, the student learns how to free his hands either by wrapping the rope around the brake-hand leg or by bringing the rope across the stomach and tying it off to the active end with a figure-eight or half hitches. He then must tie on a Prusik connected to his anchor and escape from the system. Finally, he learns to rig another anchor to replace the Prusik holding the fallen climber.

The unpleasant and complicated escape from a body belay can be eliminated by using only Sticht plate belays in the novice class. A simple overhand knot above the plate will lock it and allow tying of the Prusik. This is infinitely easier and safer for all concerned. The instructor can also demonstrate the Hedden knot with a webbing runner.

You may have noticed that no one has done any climbing so far in the course. That's because people pretty much teach themselves how to climb. The mechanics of the belay and safe procedures are what folks have to learn hands-on. Anyone paying for a course is paying to learn the skills that will allow him to climb safely on his own. These skills are the most important part of any course and they are the minimum that students must retain.

Once actual climbing begins, top roping or simple lead climbing will do the job of getting the beginners going. If you're leading, select climbs where you can see and talk to your students from your belay above. There's a lot you can teach about climbing moves while climbing, and a lot that any climber at any level can learn. That learning process is one of the great features of the sport.

GLOSSARY-INDEX

abseil: *See* **rappel**

Bachmann knot: 45–46
belay: *Verb*, to secure a rope to a fixed point. This nautical term adapted for climbing is interpreted as the action of safeguarding a climber's progress by controlling a rope attached to anchors. *Noun*, the anchor or stance where belaying is conducted. 4, 6–9, 36, 45–46, 55–57, 60–61, 64–65, 67, 70, 77, 80, 82, 87–88, 101–5, 108–9, 116, 121, 125, 127–28, 149, 153, 159–63, 179–80
bolt: Metal shaft pounded into a hole drilled into the rock to form an anchor point. Some bolts grip the hole by expansion, others by contraction. A hanger is fitted to the shaft to allow a carabiner to be clipped in. 15, 97–100, 129
bouldering: 4

carabiner: A metal snap link with a spring-loaded gate, used to attach the rope to anchors. Most carabiners are oval or D-shaped. Some have screw collars to lock the gate shut (locking carabiner, or screwgate). 35–36, 45–46, 60–61, 77, 80, 85, 91, 93, 97–100, 105, 121, 125, 127–32, 135, 146–48, 160–61, 163–64, 179–80

chock (artificial chockstone): A chockstone is a rock wedged in a crack. A runner can be threaded around it and clipped to the rope as an anchor point. British climbers used to carry stones to place in cracks. Later, they used hexagonal machine nuts found on railroad tracks, threaded through the center, as artificial chockstones. Today there are two basic types of chocks: wedges and cams. They may be active (spring-loaded) or passive. Wire, rope, or webbing can be used as chock slings. 70, 73, 77–80, 82, 84–88, 93, 103–4, 108–9, 120, 133–35, 137–39, 143–44, 146–48

double rope: Rope 9mm or less in diameter used in pairs for lead climbing. 111–14, 118, 120–21, 161

figure 8 descender: An 8-shaped metal friction device to control descent on a fixed rope (rappel). 161–64, 180
figure-eight knot (Flemish bend): A figure-eight is formed in the rope and the working end fed back through it. This is the strongest and most foolproof tie-in knot. 36, 43, 45, 77, 179
figure-eight loop: Figure-eight knot formed with a bight of rope. 43, 77, 179
Flemish bend: *See* **figure-eight knot**
free climbing: 4, 88–89, 129–30, 159
Friend: Active (spring-loaded) cam device inserted in a crack as an anchor point. 77, 88, 96, 102–3, 137–39, 143, 147

lead climbing: 4, 11–13, 46, 76, 101–5, 108–9, 152

nuts: Originally, hexagonal machine nuts found on railroad tracks and carried as artificial chockstones by British climbers. Nuts that are manufactured specifically for climbing are now